PRENATAL POSSIBILITIES

PRENATAL POSSIBILITIES

Recipes for a Healthy Pregnancy...and Beyond

PAUL QUINN

LEVEL
ZEST

First published by Level Zest 2022

Author Photo Credit: John Sharo

Recipe Photo Credit: Laura Rembold

First edition

ISBN: 978-1-68512-164-8

Cover art by Level Best Designs

This book was professionally typeset on Reedsy.
Find out more at reedsy.com

To Mom and David

Contents

III   Lunch

IV   Dinner

V   Vegetables & Salads

VI   Desserts

Foreword

Navigating pregnancy and postpartum is one of the most difficult seasons in a woman's life; mentally, emotionally, socially, and physically. There can be so many unknowns, new information, and changes occurring both to mom's body and the massive change that comes with caring for a newborn. As a registered dietitian, I specifically work with women looking to either better their prenatal and postpartum nutrition, or simply help to ditch their diet mentality and strive for a more wholesome, nutrition-centered approach. While I work with these new moms, it's not uncommon to see that many times their health and well-being become a little neglected. Using intuitive eating approaches, we're able to shift the perspective to put the priority back on nourishing their body that is giving *life*.

When I first started working with prenatal and postpartum moms, I quickly realized the importance of visualization when it comes to food and nutrition. So often the kitchen can be an overwhelming, intimidating place. For women who have become pregnant with their first, or juggling three kids running around, preparing meals is the last thing that needs to be a stressor. Food photography can help emphasize the ease of recipes and flexibility of making meals at home. This is when I became involved in the food photography side of recipe creation; to encourage women that the kitchen can be a not-so-scary place to start their health journey. For this cookbook, Dr. Quinn and I collaborated to ensure that each recipe encompassed both his vision and mission for providing nourishing, uncomplicated recipes, using affordable and accessible ingredients.

Dr. Quinn does a phenomenal job of addressing the nutritional components and benefits in his recipes, and ensures the recipes are practical, time efficient, and mom friendly. Each recipe has been hand-selected and developed to help not only support pregnancy and childbirth, but to also stay fueled and energized while she's embracing mom life.

This cookbook has a refreshing take as it shifts mom's health and nutrition back to being a priority without the fad diets and kale chips, but rather with whole, nutritious ingredients and an emphasis on education and support. Something every woman could use a little more of these days!

Laura Rembold, MS, RDN

Registered Dietitian Nutritionist

Introduction

Pregnancy is a time of infinite possibilities. There is an incredible sense of excitement, anxiety, and anticipation about the future baby (or babies!) who will arrive and what a woman will be like as a mother. More importantly, pregnancy is a time of inquiry, exploration, and discovery as women begin to learn more about their bodies, abilities, and potential. Pregnancy, then, is a time to learn and develop new habits and skills to promote health and well-being, both during pregnancy and for the future.

The internet and the availability of information have been both a blessing and a curse. On one hand, there are reputable sources available on the internet that provide factual information for women who seek answers to questions about health or pregnancy. The reputable sources, however, are few. There is too much inaccurate information available from sources that are neither reputable nor experienced. Further, there is minimal surveillance or monitoring of what is posted or by whom. Most of the information is either based on personal experience, folklore, myth, or inaccurate data that is repeated through different sources.

As a certified nurse midwife (CNM), I have spent countless hours listening to, and being with, women. I have heard their questions and provided them with answers that helped them make informed decisions about their pregnancies, care, or health choices. My intent is to do the same here: provide the most up-to-date information about nutrition, health issues, or trends surrounding pregnancy and women's general well-being. My goal is to empower women with information to make informed choices—for themselves and for their families—and provide them with tools or resources to develop healthy lifestyle habits that will stay with them far past pregnancy. Ultimately, I strive to create a culture of informed women who share healthy lifestyle choices with their children, families, and other women.

What sets me apart from the others is I come from a clinical and scientific background. I have been a nurse for close to three decades and a CNM for almost two decades. I have worked in diverse settings and had the privilege to meet, care for, and interact with the most dynamic, interesting, and insightful women. Possessing a Ph.D. in nursing, I am a scientist at heart. I have a voracious appetite for research—both performing it and evaluating it. I get excited by innovations and advances in science, medicine, nursing, and midwifery.

This cookbook is not just for pregnant women. It is intended for anyone—men, families, friends, grandparents, coworkers—who surround and support a pregnant woman or family. The recipes in this cookbook can be used by anyone who wants or needs suggestions about how to cook and eat healthier to promote a healthier lifestyle.

I made a promise to the women who allowed me into their most intimate moments physically, emotionally, and spiritually that I would honor those precious interactions by sharing what I learned from each of them with other women or families who would benefit from the lessons that, together, we co-created and benefited from. I make a similar promise here: To empower women and the significant people in their worlds with the most accurate, current information that will promote health, wellness, informed choices, and safety during the prenatal period and beyond. Join me on this journey. The possibilities are endless!

PREGNANCY NUTRITION BASICS

Pregnancy is a unique time in a woman's life. Women who eat well and exercise regularly, in conjunction with good prenatal care, are less likely to have complications during pregnancy and more likely to give birth to a healthy baby. A balanced diet and good nutrition are essential during pregnancy and while breastfeeding.

What does a healthy diet and good nutrition mean? Essentially, a balanced diet contains foods from the five major food groups. These groups include:

- Protein—from sources like meat, chicken or poultry, eggs, beans, soy products, nuts, and seeds.
- Vegetables—all kinds and all colors that are either eaten raw after thorough washing, cooked, steamed, or added as a main ingredient to a meal or side dish.
- Fruits—all kinds and all colors eaten whole or mixed into salads, main dishes, or desserts.
- Grains—from sources like whole grains, oats, breads, or pastas.
- Dairy—from sources like milk, cheese, or yogurt.

Food Group	Per Day Pre-pregnancy recommendation	Per Day Pregnancy recommendation	Per Day Breastfeeding recommendation
Protein	About 45 grams	65 to 70 grams	65 to 70 grams
Vegetables	About 2 to 3 servings (1 serving=approximately ½ cup or 75 grams)	3 to 5 servings	2 to 3 servings
Fruits	About 2 servings (1 serving=1 small piece of fruit)	2 to 4 servings	2 servings
Grains	2 to 3 servings (100% whole grain)	6 to 11 servings	6 to 8 servings
Dairy	2 to 3 servings	4 servings	3 to 4 servings

In addition, foods from the five basic food groups also provide essential vitamins and minerals (like calcium, folic acid, iron, and vitamins A through D). Sufficient amounts of vitamins and minerals in a pregnant woman's diet are believed to regulate important body functions and decrease some of the unpleasant pregnancy symptoms, like morning sickness or fatigue. Further, a pregnant woman's healthy diet is also responsible for promoting brain development in a growing baby and normal birth weight, while reducing the development of birth defects.

But how much is enough? Or how much or what serving size is considered the right amount? As a general rule, most pregnant women should take in an additional 300 calories per day (or up to 500 calories per day if breastfeeding). Calorie requirements, however, will change based upon a woman's body weight prior to pregnancy or because of conditions or complications she may develop due to her pregnancy. Additional calories, however, will contribute to weight gain. Weight gain is normal during pregnancy; how much weight a woman should gain, however, will vary, like calorie requirements, based upon a woman's pre-pregnancy weight, the conditions, the complications, or the progress of her pregnancy. For most women, a weight gain of 25 to 35 pounds is recommended.

Figure 1- Sample RDA for Pregnancy

Recommended Daily Allowance (RDA) per day for Non-Pregnancy, Pregnancy, & Breastfeeding			
	Non-Pregnant Recommendation	Pregnancy Recommendation	Breastfeeding Recommendation
Vitamin A (*not to exceed more than 10,000 IU per day)	700 mcg	770 mcg	1300 mcg
Vitamin B6	1.5 mcg	1.9 mg	2 mg
Vitamin B 12	2.4 mcg	2.6 mcg	2.8 mcg
Vitamin C	75 mg	85 mg	120 mg
Vitamin D	15 mcg	15 mcg	15 mcg
Calcium	1,000 mg	1,200-1,400 mg	1,200-1,400 mg
Folate	400 mcg	600 mcg	500 mcg
Fiber	25 g	28 g	29 g
Iron	18 mg	27 mg	20-25 mg
Magnesium	320 mg	350-360 mg	310-320 mg
Phosphorous	700 mg	700 mg	700 mg
Protein	45 g	65-70 g	65-70 g
Zinc	8 mg	11 mg	12 mg

mcg: micrograms
mg: milligrams
g: grams
IU: International Units

I

Appetizers and Snacks

Birdseed Bars

Birdseed Bars

These Birdseed Bars are super easy to make and have so many layers of complex texture, thanks to the different ingredients. Any of the ingredients can be altered so the recipe can be more savory or sweet, depending on taste. Plus, different kinds of nuts, dried fruit, or seeds can be added to give more textures or flavors.

Makes 10–12 bars

- 1 cup sesame seeds
- 1 cup sunflower seeds
- 1 cup shredded unsweetened coconut
- 1 cup nuts chopped (walnuts, pecans, or almonds)
- 1 cup raisins (brown or golden, or you can use dried cranberries, blueberries, or cherries)
- ½ cup unsalted butter
- ½ cup light brown sugar
- ¼ cup honey (natural honey works best)

1. Preheat oven to 400°.

2. Spread the sesame seeds, sunflower seeds, coconut, and nuts on a baking sheet. Roast for 6–8 minutes, until slightly browned.

3. In a large bowl, add the roasted seeds, nuts, and coconut. Add in the raisins or dried berries. Stir to combine.

4. Melt the butter, brown sugar, and honey. Stir to combine.

5. Add butter mixture to seed mixture. Stir to combine.

6. Press onto a dry baking sheet. Allow to cool fully.

7. When cooled, cut into 2x2-inch squares. Wrap in plastic wrap individually or store in an airtight container. Use wax or parchment paper on the bottom of the container and between the layers to avoid sticking.

Easy Dumplings

Easy Dumplings

Almost every culture has some form of a dumpling: a little pocket of dough filled with either a vegetable or meat that's either steamed, pan-seared, fried, baked, or boiled. This quick basic dumpling recipe can be used to build other types of fillings. These dumplings have healthy, natural ingredients without a lot of salt or fat. The basic recipe can be changed any way you like!

See dipping sauce recipe (**pp. 8-9**).

See additional dumpling recipes (**p. 9**)

Makes 8 to 10 dumplings

- 2 cups coleslaw mix (packaged coleslaw mix works best from the produce aisle)
- 3 scallions, chopped (White and light green parts only. Use the dark green parts for garnish.)
- 1½ teaspoons sesame oil
- 1 tablespoon low-sodium soy sauce
- 1½ teaspoons fresh-grated ginger
- ¼ cup bean sprouts, chopped
- ¼ cup peanuts, finely chopped (do not use if allergic)
- 15-20 dumpling or wonton wrappers

1. In a medium bowl, stir together coleslaw mix, scallions, sesame oil, soy sauce, ginger, bean sprouts, and peanuts (if using).

2. Heat a large skillet over medium heat. Add the coleslaw mixture and cook covered for 2 minutes, stirring occasionally. Uncover and cook an additional 2 to 3 minutes, until most of the liquid is evaporated and the cabbage is softened. Remove from heat.

3. Spoon 1 teaspoon of filling into the center of a dumpling or wonton wrapper. Dip your finger in water and gently moisten the edges of the wrapper. Fold the wrapper over, sealing the edges by pressing them together with your finger or a fork. Set aside on a baking sheet lined with parchment paper or foil. Repeat with remaining wrappers until mix is used.

4. Heat 1 inch of water in a large pot. Spray a steamer insert or basket with cooking spray. Add some dumplings in a single layer and steam 5 to 7 minutes, until cooked through. Repeat with remaining dumplings.

Chicken Dumplings

Add to basic dumpling recipe:

- ½ to 1 cup shredded or finely chopped cooked chicken
- 1 egg, beaten
- Black pepper to taste
- Stir these ingredients into the mixture in step 1 in the Easy Dumplings recipe.

Pork Dumplings

Add to basic dumpling recipe:

- 1 tablespoon extra-virgin olive oil
- 1 pound ground pork
- 2 cloves garlic, minced
- 1 egg beaten

1. Heat 1 tablespoon of extra-virgin olive oil in a large skillet over medium-high heat. Add the pork until brown, about 5 to 6 minutes. Add in the garlic and cook an additional 1 to 2 minutes. Remove from heat.

2. Drain any excess oil from the pan.

3. Combine the pork and 1 beaten egg into the mixture in step 1 in the Easy Dumplings recipe.

Tofu Dumplings

Add to basic dumpling recipe:

- 1 cup extra firm tofu, diced into ⅛- to ¼-inch cubes
- 1 cup mushrooms (Shiitake, brown, or white), finely chopped
- 1/2 cup minced yellow onion

Stir these ingredients into the mixture in step 1 in the Easy Dumplings recipe.

Easy Orange Dipping Sauce

- ¾ cup orange marmalade
- ¼ cup fresh-squeezed orange juice
- 2 tablespoons fresh-squeezed lemon juice
- 1 teaspoon Dijon or brown mustard

1. Microwave marmalade in a glass microwave-safe bowl for 20 to 30 seconds on high power until melted.

2. Whisk in orange juice, lemon juice, and mustard.

3. Unused portions can be reheated in the microwave on low power for 10 to 20 seconds, stirring occasionally.

Frozen Blueberry Pops

Frozen Blueberry Pops

Blueberries are packed with antioxidants that fight cell damage, plus contain vitamins C and K, fiber, other micronutrients, and water. They can be used in so many ways in recipes or simply eaten plain. In the summer, I like to make a blueberry yogurt pop that takes only a few minutes to make and is ready on-the-go.

Makes 6 pops

- 1 (16-ounce) container of blueberries, washed
- 1 tablespoon fresh lemon juice
- 4 tablespoons honey (natural is best)
- 1¾ cups plain, nonfat Greek yogurt
- ½ cup granola or crushed cereal of your choice (optional)
- Wooden craft sticks and ice pop molds (or use any ice pop mold kit you have)

1. In a food processor, add the blueberries, lemon juice, and 2 tablespoons honey. Pulse until the mixture is mostly smooth but not fully puréed.

2. In a medium bowl, stir together the yogurt and the remaining 2 tablespoons of honey until combined.

3. Fill the molds ¾ full of alternating tablespoonfuls of the blueberry mixture and the yogurt mixture. Use the back of a flat knife to gently stir the mixture within the mold to create a marble effect.

4. Each mold can be topped with granola or crushed cereal (optional).

5. Insert a wooden stick into each mold. You may need plastic wrap to support the stick if not using granola or cereal. Freeze until solid.

6. When ready, the mold may need to be run under warm water for a few seconds to loosen.

This recipe can also be made with just the blueberries: Use two 16-ounce packages of blueberries, 2 tablespoons of lemon juice, and the 4 tablespoons of honey. Follow the same process to prepare the blueberry mixture. Add only the blueberry mixture to the ice pop molds and omit ending with granola or crushed cereal. Insert the wooden sticks into the molds and freeze until solid.

Ginger Vanilla Crunch Bars

Ginger Vanilla Crunch Bars

This recipe uses the warm spice of ginger to create a unique flavor and texture. There's plenty of crunch to complement the chewiness from the coconut. Since cereal and oat provide the bulk for these bars, you can also make this gluten-free. Don't have cereal? Just add in extra oats. You can easily change up the nuts or fruits you use to make it your own.

Makes 12 bars

- 1 cup old-fashioned rolled oats (not instant)
- ½ cup of your favorite flaked cereal (cornflakes, bran flakes)
- ½ cup chopped almonds
- ½ cup shredded coconut
- ¼ cup crystallized ginger, chopped into small pieces
- ¼ cup butter
- ½ cup pure maple syrup or natural honey
- 2 tablespoons milk (whole, 2%, soy, almond, or cashew)
- ½ cup chopped, pitted dates
- 2 scoops protein powder (plain or vanilla flavor)

1. Preheat oven to 325°.

2. Line a 9x9- or 8x8-inch baking dish with parchment paper.

3. In a large bowl, add oats, cereal, almonds, coconut, and ginger. Stir to combine.

4. In a medium saucepan over medium heat, combine the butter, maple syrup or honey, milk, dates, and protein powder. Stir occasionally.

5. When butter mixture is melted and smooth, pour over the oat mixture. Stir to combine.

6. Spread the oat mix into the prepared pan. Use water or vegetable oil spray on your hands to help spread and press the mix evenly into the pan and into the corners.

7. Bake for 20 minutes. Cool completely before cutting into squares or triangles. Store in an airtight container or wrap the bars individually in plastic wrap for up to a week. Freeze in an airtight container for up to 2 months.

Healthy Sliders

Healthy Sliders

This recipe takes away all the fatty cuts of meat found in traditional sliders and instead uses a turkey patty packed with flavor and protein. Placing the onion in the food processor is a quick trick to keeping these turkey patties moist, while giving them an extra boost of flavor. Try your favorite toppings or add extra vegetables on top. You can even use lettuce leaves instead of a bun for extra flavor or crunch. These sliders are great plain but try mixing and matching different toppings to elevate the flavor.

Makes 12 sliders

- 1 small yellow onion
- 1 pound ground lean turkey
- ¾ cup chopped cilantro or parsley
- ½ teaspoon salt
- ¼ teaspoon garlic powder
- ¼ teaspoon fresh black pepper
- Crisp lettuce leaves or small slider rolls
- Optional: vegetables or spreads

1. Peel and slice the onion into quarters. Place the onion quarters in a food processor or blender and pulse until the onion is finely chopped and releases some of its liquid.

2. In a large bowl, combine the ground turkey, onion, cilantro or parsley, salt, garlic powder, and black pepper until combined.

3. Using your hands, take about ¼ cup of the turkey mixture and form a small, round patty. Do not over mix. Make a tiny dimple in the center of each patty.

4. Cook the patties:

- On grill over medium heat, cook for 2 to 3 minutes per side.
- In a skillet over medium-high heat, cook until the patties are cooked through, about 5 minutes each side.
- In a preheated oven at 350° for about 25 minutes, until the patties are cooked through.

5. Assemble the sliders while warm on crisp lettuce leaves or on small slider rolls. Top with your favorite vegetables or spreads.

Incredible Flatbreads

Incredible Flatbreads

Flatbreads are the ultimate in versatility: they take no time to make, and the recipe can be doubled or tripled, depending on the number of people you're serving. This recipe is so easy you can easily make it your own. Change up the flavors and use what you have on hand in your refrigerator or from your garden or what's available at your local grocery store.

Makes 4 to 6 servings per flatbread

Basic Flatbread

- 1 cup all-purpose flour (or gluten-free flour or whole-wheat flour) plus additional for dusting the rolling surface
- ½ teaspoon salt
- ¼ to ½ teaspoon baking powder (more baking powder makes a fluffier flatbread with dough bubbles)
- ½ cup plain yogurt

1. Whisk flour, salt and baking powder in a medium bowl.

2. Add in yogurt and stir until combined.

3. Lightly dust a work surface with flour and turn out the dough onto the floured surface.

4. Knead dough until smooth, about 1 to 2 minutes.

5. Divide dough into 2 pieces. Wrap in plastic wrap and allow to rest in refrigerator or cool place for 15 to 30 minutes. (If doubling or tripling the dough, the number of cut pieces will also increase.)

6. Roll 1 piece of the dough on the lightly floured surface to 1/8-inch

thickness. Sprinkle with flour to prevent sticking.

7. Heat a medium skillet or a cast iron skillet over medium heat. Cook flatbread until golden and fluffy with some dark charred spots, about 2 minutes per side.

Spinach and Mushroom Flatbread

Try adding pieces of diced grilled, baked, or poached chicken if desired

- 1 tablespoon extra-virgin olive oil
- 8 ounces baby Portobello mushrooms (or white or shiitake mushrooms)
- 1 shallot, chopped
- ½ cup chopped spinach
- ¼ cup shredded Mozzarella cheese
- ¼ cup grated Parmesan cheese

1. Preheat oven to 350°. Line a baking sheet with parchment paper and top with 2 flatbreads.

2. In a large skillet, heat extra-virgin olive oil over medium heat. Add mushrooms and shallot and cook 2 to 3 minutes, until mushrooms are fragrant and tender, and the shallot is wilted.

3. Add spinach and sauté 1 to 2 minutes.

4. Spread mushroom and spinach mixture on flatbread and top with mozzarella cheese.

5. Bake 10 to 12 minutes, until bubbly.

6. Allow to cool slightly and serve.

Vegetarian Flatbread

- 1 medium sweet potato, peeled and diced into 1-inch cubes
- 1 medium yellow onion, peeled and diced into 1-inch cubes
- 1 medium green zucchini, diced into 1-inch cubes
- 2 carrots, peeled and diced into 1-inch cubes
- 1 beet or medium purple potato, peeled and diced into 1-inch cubes
- 1 parsnip, peeled and diced into 1-inch cubes
- 2 tablespoons extra-virgin olive oil
- ½ teaspoon salt
- ½ teaspoon pepper
- Optional: ½ cup fresh-grated Parmesan cheese or Fontina cheese

1. Heat oven to 350°. Line a baking sheet with parchment paper.

2. In a large bowl, combine all diced vegetables, salt, and pepper and stir to combine.

3. Spread vegetables onto baking sheet. Bake 10 to 15 minutes, until slightly browned, stirring midway through baking.

4. Remove from heat and cool slightly.

5. Line second baking sheet with parchment paper and top with 2 flatbreads.

6. Top each flatbread with browned, roasted vegetables. Sprinkle with cheeses, if using.

7. Bake 10 to 12 minutes, until vegetables are softened and caramelized, and cheese (if using) is melted and bubbly. Remove from oven and cool slightly. Slice into 4 equal pieces for easier serving.

Pesto, Spinach & Cheese Flatbread

- · 1 tablespoon extra-virgin olive oil
- · 1 cup spinach, finely chopped
- · 1 clove garlic, minced
- · ½ cup fresh Mozzarella, shredded
- · ¼ cup fresh-grated Parmesan cheese
- · 1-2 teaspoons pesto (try the recipe for Perfect Pesto!)

1. Preheat oven to 350°. Line a baking sheet with parchment paper. Place 2 prepared flatbread crusts on the lined baking sheet.

2. In a medium skillet, heat extra-virgin olive oil over medium heat.

3. Add spinach and garlic and sauté until wilted, about 1 to 2 minutes.

4. Spread the spinach mixture on the flatbread crusts.

5. Top with Mozzarella and Parmesan cheeses.

6. Drizzle pesto evenly over flatbreads.

7. Bake 12 to 13 minutes, until the top is golden and bubbly. Remove from oven and allow to cool slightly before slicing or serving.

Peanut Butter Bites

Peanut Butter Bites

Peanut butter contains about 4 grams of protein per serving. Make these super-easy peanut butter bites that work well to fight off hunger and satisfy any craving for a healthy, salty snack.

Makes 16–18 peanut butter bites

- 1 cup old-fashioned oats (not instant)
- ½ cup peanut butter (creamy, crunchy, or natural)
- ⅓ cup natural honey
- ¼ cup chia seeds (optional)
- 1 teaspoon vanilla (optional for a little more sweetness)
- ⅔ cup toasted, unsweetened coconut (optional)

1. Mix all ingredients together in a medium bowl. Refrigerate mixture for 30 to 60 minutes.

2. Take a tablespoon-sized amount of mix and gently roll into a ball. If the mix is not sticking (which may happen, depending on the peanut butter you use or the humidity) add more honey, drops at a time, or an additional dab of peanut butter until the mix comes together in a ball easily.

3. Store in an airtight container in the refrigerator for up to 2 weeks. These can be kept longer in the freezer.

Peanut Butter Thins

Peanut Butter Thins

These are truly unique. They're not a cookie but not quite a cracker. They are the perfect combination of texture and taste! I add in chia seeds to provide an additional boost of Omega 3 and other nutrients plus some extra texture. These thins take no time to bake. The trick is making a thin layer on the bottom of the baking dish so they stay crispy. Don't overbake them because they can burn quickly, but don't undercook them or they'll be too chewy.

Makes 16 to 18 thins

- 1 cup whole-wheat flour
- ¼ cup rolled oats
- 2 teaspoons chia seeds
- ½ teaspoon salt
- ¼ teaspoon cinnamon
- ⅓ cup natural or creamy peanut butter (any brand)
- ⅓ cup packed light brown sugar
- 2½ tablespoons extra-virgin olive oil
- 1 large egg white

1. Preheat oven to 350°. Line a 9x12 baking dish with aluminum foil, allowing the foil to overhang about an inch on all sides. Spray the foil-lined baking dish lightly with nonstick vegetable spray.

2. In a large bowl, combine the whole-wheat flour, oats, chia seeds, salt, and cinnamon. Set aside.

3. In a medium bowl, combine peanut butter, brown sugar, extra-virgin olive oil, and egg white. Beat with an electric mixer until creamy, about 2 to 3 minutes.

4. Add the flour mixture and mix on low speed until all the ingredients are combined and resemble wet sand that easily sticks together.

5. Turn the dough into the prepared baking dish and press it down into a thin layer, including into the corners.

6. Bake until golden brown and firm, about 25 to 30 minutes. Remove from the oven and allow to cool completely. Using the foil as handles, lift the cooled thins out of the baking dish and onto a cutting board. Slice into 2-inch squares or pieces.

Perfect Pickles

Perfect Pickles

Pregnant women often crave salty or vinegary types of foods that have texture or a crunch. Pickles are an ideal snack to satisfy those types of cravings. These are the easiest recipes to make homemade pickles that are low in sodium, have no additional preservatives, can be either sweet or acidic, and can be kept on hand for a snack emergency. Any crunchy vegetable can be added, like slices of carrots or radishes to add extra texture and taste.

Makes 3 medium jars

- 4 cups water
- 2 cups white vinegar
- 1½ tablespoon kosher salt
- 1 teaspoon white sugar
- 4 cups sliced pickling cucumbers (either ¼-inch circles or in spears)
- 1 small sweet onion, thinly sliced
- 4 garlic cloves, peeled and sliced
- 1 tablespoon mustard seeds (optional)
- 1 tablespoon whole black peppercorns (optional)

1. Prepare the brine: Combine water, vinegar, salt, and sugar in a medium saucepan. Bring to a boil over medium-high heat and stir until all the salt and sugar is dissolved. Remove from heat and allow to cool to room temperature.

2. Add the cucumber slices to jars or containers with tight sealing lids. Do not over pack them and leave room for them to float easily in the brine. Add in the onion, garlic, and mustard seeds, if using, and peppercorns, if using.

3. Add enough cooled brine to cover the cucumber slices. Seal the containers and store in the refrigerator for 1 week. Pickles should last about 4 to 6

weeks in the refrigerator.

Sweet Pickles

Makes 2 medium jars

- 2 cups sliced cucumbers (either ¼-inch discs or spears)
- 1 small sweet onion, thinly sliced
- ½ cup water
- 1 cup apple cider vinegar
- 1 teaspoon salt
- ½ cup white sugar
- ⅛ cup packed brown sugar
- 1 teaspoon mustard seeds (optional)
- 1 teaspoon celery seeds (optional)
- 1 teaspoon white peppercorns (optional)

1. Place sliced cucumbers and onion in heat-safe jars or containers. Do not over pack; leave enough room for the cucumbers to float easily in the brine.

2. Prepare the brine: Combine water, vinegar, salt, and sugars in a medium saucepan. Bring to a boil over medium-high heat. Reduce heat and simmer for 5 minutes.

3. Pour the hot brine over the cucumbers and onions. Allow to cool.

4. Add in the seeds and peppercorns, if using. Seal the container and refrigerator for at least 2 hours before serving.

5. Store for up to 2 months in the refrigerator.

Polenta Fritters

Polenta Fritters

Polenta is a staple in Italian cuisine. With its rich corn flavor, polenta is versatile enough to pair with any meal. However, it can also be made into a savory snack with just a few simple ingredients. These fritters can be made any size. This snack provides about 9 grams of protein and fiber. It pairs well with a variety of dips or toppings, like salsa, marinara sauce, carrot hummus, cheeses, or a dollop of low-fat sour cream. A batch of these fritters can be made in advance and reheated later, or they can be served warm and fresh from the griddle.

Makes 14 to 16

- 1 cup instant polenta
- 1 cup whole-wheat flour
- 1½ teaspoons baking powder
- ½ teaspoon salt
- 1½ cups plain Greek yogurt
- 4 tablespoons extra-virgin olive oil
- ¼ cup natural maple syrup or honey
- 2 eggs, separated
- 1 10-ounce package of frozen yellow corn, thawed and drained
- Vegetable oil spray for the griddle or skillet

1. In a large bowl, combine polenta, whole-wheat flour, baking powder, and salt.

2. In a medium bowl, whisk Greek yogurt, extra-virgin olive oil, syrup or honey, and egg yolks.

3. Stir yogurt mixture into flour mixture and stir until combined.

4. In a medium bowl, beat the egg whites with an electric mixer until stiff

peaks form. Fold into the batter gently. Fold in the thawed corn.

5. Coat a griddle or large skillet with the vegetable spray over medium heat. Drop rounded tablespoons of batter onto the griddle or skillet and cook 3 to 4 minutes on each side until the fritters are golden brown and crisp. Transfer the fritters to a plate and keep warm or allow to cool and store in an airtight container in the refrigerator up to 1 week or freeze for up to 1 month.

Roasted Chickpeas

Roasted Chickpeas

These make a perfect, crunchy snack because they contain the right amount of flavor, vitamins, nutrients, and fiber. They are easy to make, and you can vary the recipe by adding in other flavors.

Makes 1½ cups

- 1 can (12 ounces) chickpeas (Garbanzo Beans), drained
- 2 tablespoons olive oil (extra virgin is best)
- Salt & pepper to taste

1. Preheat oven to 450°.

2. Blot the chickpeas with a paper towel to dry.

3. Mix chickpeas, olive oil, salt, and pepper to taste in a bowl.

4. Spread chickpeas on a baking sheet and bake 30 to 40 minutes, until brown and crunchy. Use caution toward the end of baking to avoid burning.

5. Allow to cool. Store in an airtight container for up to 1 week.

Other flavors can be added to these—try ¼ to ½ teaspoon of garlic powder, cayenne, cinnamon, cardamom, rosemary, garam masala, coriander, and cumin to taste when mixing chickpeas with the olive oil. Or, after baking, sprinkle lightly with parsley and fresh-grated Parmesan cheese.

Salt & Vinegar Zucchini Chips

Salt & Vinegar Zucchini Chips

What is the one snack I promote that offers a lot of flavor plus an extra bonus of fiber? Zucchini chips! They're healthy, easy, and affordable. A big batch of these keeps well in an airtight container for several days.

Makes 24-30 chips

- 1 large zucchini
- 2 tablespoons olive oil
- ½ teaspoon salt
- 2 tablespoons malt vinegar
- ¼ teaspoon paprika

1. Preheat oven to 225°.

2. Use a mandolin to slice the zucchini into discs, approximately ⅛-inch thick. (Careful! Mandolins can be dangerous if not used according to the manufacturer's directions.) If you don't have a mandolin, you can slice the zucchini with a food processor or by hand. It's important to keep them thin but not too thin that they will burn.)

3. Place the discs of zucchini onto paper towels in a row. Cover and pat dry with an additional paper towel.

4. Mix the olive oil, salt, and malt vinegar in a bowl.

5. Line baking sheets with parchment paper.

6. Brush the zucchini discs (or dip) with the oil/vinegar/salt mixture and place on the parchment-lined baking sheet.

7. Bake for 1 hour and 15 minutes. Check the chips occasionally to insure

they aren't burning.

8. Remove from the oven and sprinkle with paprika. Allow to cool completely. Store in an airtight container for up to a week.

For a different taste:

Omit the vinegar and paprika. Follow the directions and, at the end, sprinkle with ¼ cup fresh-grated Parmesan cheese and parsley. Or sprinkle fresh-grated orange zest for a crisp, bright taste.

Try a crack of fresh-grated black pepper added to the oil, vinegar, and salt.

Omit the vinegar and paprika and substitute ¼ teaspoon Chinese 5-Spice powder after they're baked for a mild Asian flavor.

Omit the vinegar and paprika and substitute ¼ teaspoon Italian seasoning at the end.

Craving something sweet? Omit the vinegar, salt, and paprika and sprinkle the chips with 1/2 teaspoon of sugar, mixed with ¼ teaspoon cinnamon or cardamom.

Shortcut Shortbread Crackers

Shortcut Shortbread Crackers

Crackers, while delicious, aren't always healthy. Even crackers that are labeled whole grain or multigrain often contain sodium, fats, or preservatives that make them not the healthiest option to choose. The options for eating healthy snacks are limited, but it's so easy to create your own! These crackers pair with anything: cheese, fruit, spreads, or vegetables. They're perfect for a party or for women who experience morning sickness.

Makes 12 to 14 crackers

- 1 stick (¼ pound) unsalted butter, softened
- 1¼ cup all-purpose flour
- ¼ teaspoon kosher salt

Options:

- 3 ounces fresh-grated Parmesan cheese
- 1½ teaspoons fresh thyme, diced
- 1½ teaspoons fresh rosemary, diced
- 1 teaspoon vanilla
- ½ teaspoon cinnamon

1. In a stand-up electric mixer with the paddle attachment, mix butter until creamy.

2. Add flour and salt. Mix until combined.

3. Dump dough onto lightly floured surface and roll into a 12-inch log.

4. Wrap log in plastic wrap and freeze 30 to 45 minutes.

5. Preheat oven to 350°.

6. Cut the dough log crosswise into ½-inch thick slices.

7. Place dough slices on a sheet pan or baking sheet and bake 20 to 22 minutes, until lightly browned.

8. Remove from oven and cool. Store in an airtight container for up to 10 days.

Strawberry Protein Bars

Strawberry Protein Bars

These bars have only 5 ingredients and are so easy to make. Unlike commercially made snack products, these bars are high in nutrients like iron, calcium, and potassium. They're naturally high in protein, thanks to the almond butter, but protein powders can be added to give it an extra boost. These can be eaten fresh or frozen and used later. They are also gluten-free and vegan.

Makes 10 to 12 bars

- 2 cups rolled oats (not instant)
- 2½ cups strawberries (fresh or frozen and thawed), mashed
- 3 tablespoons maple syrup (Grade A best)
- 4 tablespoons almond butter
- ¼ cup almond milk (flavored or unsweetened)

Optional:

- 1 cup vanilla or peanut butter protein powder
- 2 ounces of dark chocolate,chopped or chips
- Sliced almonds, toasted

1. Preheat oven to 350°.

2. Line an 8- or 10-inch square baking pan with parchment paper.

3. In a food processor, process half the oats (1¼ cup) for 2 to 5 pulses. Do not over pulse or turn it into a fine powder mix.

4. Combine all ingredients in a large bowl. Mix well. If using, add in any optional ingredients and stir to combine.

5. Bake 20 to 25 minutes, or until a toothpick inserted in the middle comes out moist with only a few small crumbs.

6. Once cooled, use parchment to remove from baking pan. Slice into 1- or 2-inch bars or squares and wrap individually with plastic wrap or store in an airtight container or plastic sealing bag.

7. Optional: Sprinkle the top with additional chocolate or toasted nuts for extra taste and texture.

Toasted Almonds

Toasted Almonds

Nuts, especially almonds, are one of the best snack foods. One ounce (28 grams) or a small handful of almonds is high in protein (about 6 grams) and fiber (3.5 grams) and the "good" kind of fat (monounsaturated). They are naturally low in carbohydrates, high in natural antioxidants, and high in vitamins and minerals like magnesium, copper, zinc, vitamins B2 and E, and phosphorous. Roasting nuts brings out their flavors and these recipes give you easy ways to prepare almonds—from sweet and salty to lightly sugar-coated. Try chopping them and sprinkling them over salads and roasted or steamed vegetables or stirred into yogurt or sprinkling some over hot oatmeal or farina or make them into small packets to keep in your bag, pocket, or in a lunch box. These make a perfect homemade gift to send your guests home with or put them in decorative jars for a homemade holiday gift.

Sweet and Salty Nuts

Makes 8 servings

- 2 cups whole, raw almonds
- $\frac{1}{2}$ teaspoon salt
- $\frac{1}{8}$ teaspoon cayenne pepper or Chinese 5-Spice powder (optional)
- 4 tablespoons honey (Natural or local honey is best)
- 2 tablespoons light olive oil

1. Preheat oven to 350°. Line a baking sheet with parchment paper.

2. In a large bowl, add the almonds, salt, cayenne pepper or Chinese 5-Spice powder if using, honey, and light olive oil. Stir to combine.

3. Transfer the nuts to the prepared baking sheet and evenly spread them out. Bake 12 to 14 minutes, until the honey caramelizes and the almonds

are fragrant.

4. Remove from the oven and allow to cool.

5. Store in an airtight container for up to 2 weeks.

Maple Cinnamon Almonds

Makes 8 servings

- 2 cups whole raw almonds
- 1 teaspoon cinnamon
- ½ teaspoon salt
- 4 tablespoons natural maple syrup
- 1 teaspoon light olive oil

1. Preheat oven to 350°. Line a baking sheet with parchment paper.

2. In a large bowl, add the almonds, cinnamon, salt, maple syrup, and light olive oil. Stir to combine.

3. Transfer the nuts to the prepared baking sheet and evenly spread them out. Bake 12 to 14 minutes, until the honey caramelizes and the almonds are fragrant.

4. Remove from the oven and allow to cool.

5. Store in an airtight container for up to 2 weeks.

Sugar Coated Almonds

Makes 8 servings

- ¾ cup white sugar
- ¼ cup packed brown sugar
- ¼ teaspoon salt
- ½ cup water
- 2 cups whole raw almonds

1. In a small bowl, combine the white sugar, brown sugar, and salt. Mix well. Set aside.

2. In a large skillet or medium nonstick saucepan, heat the water to a low simmer. Do not boil.

3. Add the sugar mixture and stir to combine. Bring to a low boil and add the almonds, stirring to evenly coat the almonds.

4. Cook over medium-high heat 12 to 15 minutes, until the liquid reduces and begins to thicken, stirring often.

5. When the liquid is almost fully reduced, stir constantly. The liquid will become a flaky, crystallized coating on the nuts. Remove from the heat.

6. Spread the nuts on a baking sheet and allow them to cool completely.

7. Store in an airtight container or a resealable bag for 1 to 2 weeks.

Versatile Smoothies

Versatile Smoothies

Smoothies can be used anytime, anywhere, to satisfy hunger and provide necessary nutrients. All you need is a few ingredients, a blender, a large glass, and a straw and you're on your way. Try different combinations of your favorite flavors and add in sweet or savory flavors to your own taste.

The Basic Smoothie

- 1 cup plain nonfat or Greek yogurt
- 1 banana (room temperature or cut into slices and frozen)
- ½ cup of orange juice (fresh is best but store-bought, commercial orange juice is fine)
- 6 frozen strawberries (put a bag of fresh strawberries in the freezer or keep a bag of store-bought whole frozen strawberries in your freezer for this recipe)

1. Blend for 20 seconds. Scrape the sides of the blender and blend again for an additional 15 seconds.

Berry Smoothie

Makes 2 servings

- 1 cup frozen raspberries
- ½ cup fresh cut strawberries (or 4-6 whole frozen strawberries)
- ¾ cup unsweetened almond milk
- 1½ tablespoons natural honey
- 2 teaspoons fresh ginger (or ¼ to ½ teaspoon of dried ginger)
- 1 teaspoon of ground flax seed or 1 tablespoon of chia seeds (for protein)
- 2 teaspoons of fresh lemon juice (or several drops of commercial lemon juice) to taste

1. Blend all ingredients, except the lemon juice, until smooth. Add lemon juice sparingly to taste.

Banana Ginger Smoothie

Makes 2 servings

- 1 banana, sliced and frozen (slice the banana into 1-inch slices then freeze)
- ¾ cup vanilla-flavored Greek yogurt (or plain if desired)
- ½ cup unsweetened almond milk
- 1 tablespoon natural honey
- ½ teaspoon fresh-grated ginger

1. Blend all ingredients until smooth.

Carrot-Mango Smoothie

Makes 2 servings

- 2-3 carrots, peeled and chopped
- 1 kiwi, peeled
- 1 mango, peeled and pitted (or 1 cup frozen mango)
- 1 tablespoon flaxseed or chia seed
- 3 tablespoons unsalted cashews
- 1 cup water
- 1 cup ice

1. Blend all ingredients until smooth.

Avocado-Herb Smoothie

Makes 2 servings

- 1 avocado, peeled and pitted
- ½ cup fresh parsley
- ½ cup fresh basil
- Pinch of fresh rosemary (about 1 to 4 rosemary leaves)
- Pinch of thyme (about 6 to 10 small leaves)
- 1 cup water
- Dashes of salt and pepper
- Splash of olive oil

1. Blend all ingredients until smooth.

2. Serve in small glasses with whole-wheat or whole-grain crackers.

II

Breakfast

A.M. Avocados

A.M. Avocados

Avocados contain fiber, potassium, and Omega-3 fatty acids and are naturally low in sugar. That makes them a perfect main course or meat substitute for women (or the family). Since breakfast is the most important meal of the day, this recipe is packed with protein from eggs and the avocado. This meal will ward off hunger and keep you feeling full for several hours.

Makes 4 servings

- 4 ripe avocados
- 4 medium eggs
- 2 slices cooked bacon, crumbled (optional)
- Parsley, chives, or other chopped herbs to garnish
- Salt & pepper to taste

1. Preheat oven to 425°.

2. Slice avocados in half and remove the pit. Scoop out about 1 to 2 tablespoons of avocado flesh from the center to make a shallow well that will allow the egg to fit snugly in the center.

3. Place the avocados in a small baking dish or on a baking sheet.

4. Crack an egg into the center of each avocado. Tip: Try to put the egg yolk in first, then fill the egg white in around the yolk. It's OK if the egg white spills over onto the avocado or down the sides.

5. Bake 15 to 20 minutes.

6. Garnish with crumbled bacon, parsley, and chives (or any fresh herbs you like), Salt & pepper to taste. Try toasted triangles of tortillas or pita bread on the side.

Blueberry Bliss Breakfast Bars

Blueberry Bliss Breakfast Bars

This recipe is high in protein, is gluten-free, and can satisfy vegetarians. The different ingredients provide texture and flavor, and the recipe is quick to prepare and involves no baking.

Makes 8 servings (1 large bar or 2 small bars=1 serving)

- 1½ cups rolled oats (not instant!)
- ¾ cup whole, unsalted almonds
- ½ cup pistachios, shelled and chopped
- ¼ cup sunflower seeds
- ¼ cup walnuts, chopped
- ⅓ cup flax seeds
- ¼ cup chia seeds
- ¾ cup dried blueberries
- ¼ cup pepitas (toasted pumpkin) seeds
- ⅓ cup honey or pure maple syrup
- ¼ cup unsweetened applesauce
- ½ teaspoon fresh-grated lemon zest
- 1 cup almond or sunflower butter

1. Line an 8x8-inch baking pan with parchment paper, leaving enough paper to overhang the edges.

2. Add the oats, almonds, pistachios, sunflower seeds, walnuts, flax seeds, chia seeds, dried blueberries, and pepitas in a large bowl. Stir to combine.

3. Add the honey or maple syrup, applesauce, and lemon zest. Stir to combine.

4. Add almond or sunflower butter and stir to combine.

5. Place in the prepared pan. Press the mix down firmly with your hand and offset spatula or the back of a ½ cup-sized measuring cup to distribute mix evenly in the pan.

6. Place the pan with the mixture into the freezer for 1 to 2 hours, until firmly set.

7. Remove from freezer. Lift the mixture out of the pan, using the overhanging edges of the parchment paper. Peel the paper away gently.

8. Slice into 8 long bars or into 16 smaller bars.

9. Serve at room temperature or wrap each piece individually.

Breakfast Sweet Potatoes

Breakfast Sweet Potatoes

Sweet potatoes make an ideal complement to any breakfast! Unlike white potatoes, sweet potatoes are full of nutrients because of their color: vitamin A, niacin, vitamin B6, phosphorous, copper, potassium, and, most importantly, fiber. Even better, sweet potatoes are easy to prepare and combine with so many ingredients to make them a truly versatile option for breakfast. Paired with eggs or any kind of bacon, it provides protein and flavor that will keep a woman, or family, feeling full for hours.

Makes 4 servings

- 2 sweet potatoes, medium to large size
- ¼ cup extra-virgin olive oil (or ⅓ cup ghee or butter if preferred)
- Salt & pepper to taste
- 4 slices turkey bacon
- Dash cinnamon
- 4 eggs
- ½ cup thinly sliced scallions
- Optional: natural maple syrup, honey, Greek yogurt, or extra crumbles of bacon

1. Preheat oven to 400°.

2. Line a baking sheet with aluminum foil or parchment paper.

3. Clean sweet potatoes and toss with extra-virgin olive oil. Poke holes with a fork all around the sweet potato to create air vents and season with salt and pepper.

4. Bake 1 hour or until soft on the inside.

5. While the potatoes are baking, cook the bacon until crisp. Drain the bacon

on paper towels and set aside. Crumble when cooled.

6. Cut cooked and cooled sweet potatoes in half with a sharp knife. Gently scoop out the inside of the potatoes into a bowl, using a spoon.

7. Mix sweet potato pulp, bacon, cinnamon, and salt and pepper as needed.

8. Fill each potato half with filling. Make a well large enough to hold an egg.

9. Crack an egg into the center well of each sweet potato and bake for an additional 15 to 20 minutes, until the yolk is cooked (cook less if a runny yolk is preferred or longer if you prefer a drier, more stiff yolk).

10. Season with additional salt and pepper if needed, garnish with scallions or drizzle with natural maple syrup, honey, or Greek yogurt, or add extra crumbles of bacon.

Cornmeal Waffles

Cornmeal Waffles

This recipe uses cornmeal to add more flavor and texture. These waffles bake up to golden brown with the same light crisp edges but have no grease or wet texture and no extra sugar. They pair perfectly with fresh fruit, pure maple syrup or natural local honey, a light dusting of powdered sugar, or a sprinkle of turbinado sugar. These waffles store well in a resealable bag in the refrigerator for several days or can be frozen up to a month.

Makes 6 to 8 servings

- 1¼ cup all-purpose flour
- 1¾ cup yellow cornmeal
- 1 tablespoon baking powder
- ¼ teaspoon salt
- 1 tablespoon packed brown sugar
- 2 cups milk (Almond, 2%, or whole)
- 2½ teaspoons light vegetable oil
- 2 eggs, beaten
- 2 teaspoons vanilla

1. Preheat waffle maker to medium or 300° to 350° setting.

2. In a medium bowl, combine flour, cornmeal, baking powder, salt, and brown sugar. Mix well.

3. In a second medium bowl (or in a blender), whisk milk, vegetable oil, eggs, and vanilla until combined.

4. Pour wet ingredients into the dry flour mixture and stir to combine.

5. Pour 1 cup or 1 large ladleful of batter onto the center of the preheated waffle iron. Allow the batter to slowly settle into the iron's grooves before

closing the lid to bake the waffle.

6. Bake until golden, according to waffle iron manufacturer's instructions, typically 5 to 6 minutes.

7. Lift lid carefully and allow steam to escape. Remove waffle to a plate and repeat the steps for the next waffle. Serve with the topping of your choice.

Cottage Cheese Toast

Cottage Cheese Toast

Cottage cheese is high in protein, B vitamins, calcium, iron, zinc, and phosphorous. It's also low in cholesterol, calories, and sodium, so it's a go-to option for anyone. Here's a fast, easy breakfast that pregnant women, or anyone, can enjoy. The energy this meal provides will get you through the morning and keep you feeling full until it's time for a mid-morning snack or lunch.

Makes 2 servings

- ½ cup cottage cheese
- 1 tablespoon honey
- 1 teaspoon cinnamon
- 2 slices of multigrain bread, toasted
- Sliced peaches, bananas, strawberries, black or red plums, red grapes, or green or McIntosh apples
- Optional: additional honey, natural maple syrup, turbinado sugar, wheat germ, chia seeds, or additional cinnamon or nutmeg

1. Mix cottage cheese, honey, and cinnamon until smooth.

2. Spread cottage cheese mixture on warm toast.

3. Top with fruit slices—it can be slices of one fruit or a combination of several fruits.

4. If desired, drizzle with additional honey, natural maple syrup, ¼ teaspoon of turbinado sugar, wheat germ, chia seeds, or additional cinnamon or nutmeg.

Easiest Pancakes Ever

Easiest Pancakes Ever

This recipe adds in peanut butter for extra protein and oats for extra fiber and is sweetened with applesauce instead of sugar. The best part: instead of standing over a griddle trying to flip pancakes, these go right in the oven and come out perfect each time! Make several batches of these pancakes and leave them in the refrigerator or freezer between sheets of wax paper. They're perfect to reheat or use as a dessert with a dollop of ice cream, whipped cream, or a drizzle of chocolate syrup or honey.

Makes 8–10 pancakes

- ¼ cup creamy or chunky peanut butter
- ¼ cup unsweetened applesauce
- 1 egg
- 1 egg white
- 3 tablespoons old-fashioned rolled oats (not the quick-cooking kind)
- 1 cup all-purpose flour (add more if the mix is too loose or watery)
- ¼ teaspoon baking soda
- ¼ teaspoon cinnamon
- ½ teaspoon vanilla
- Pinch of salt

1. Preheat oven to 350°.

2. Line 2 baking sheets with parchment paper.

3. Combine all ingredients in a large bowl.

4. Allow the mixture to sit so oats can soften, 5 to 10 minutes.

5. Scoop batter in 3- or 4-inch circles onto parchment-lined baking sheets (or use smaller circles if desired).

6. Bake 10 to 12 minutes, until pancake is fluffy and the top is browned.

7. Cool 1 to 2 minutes then enjoy with your favorite topping or fruit.

Kale & Feta Toast

Kale & Feta Toast

This recipe elevates toast to a more savory, delicious combination that everyone has been asking for. Feta cheese offers a tangy, yet creamy bite. A little feta goes a long way. A few crumbles are often enough to provide a salty note to any dish. The kale, sautéed lightly with a touch of garlic, adds a touch of natural sweetness and texture that pairs well with, and mellows, the feta. This dish is delicious on its own, but you can easily add in any style of eggs and have a new take on eggs Florentine. Or add in some small pieces of leftover chicken or thin slices of beef or pork to add in more savory flavors.

Makes 2 servings

- 2 slices of multigrain bread with seeds (or try gluten-free, rye, pumpernickel, or wheat bread or a multigrain English muffin)
- 2 teaspoons extra-virgin olive oil
- 2½ cups chopped kale, stems removed (approximately 1 bunch of kale)
- 1 garlic clove, minced
- ¼ teaspoon salt
- Dash of fresh ground black pepper
- 2 ounces feta cheese, crumbled
- Optional: 2 eggs (poached, scrambled, fried, or hard boiled and sliced), cooked chicken (crumbled or diced small), steak or pork sliced thin

1. Toast bread as desired; set aside.

2. Heat extra-virgin olive oil in a large skillet over medium–high heat.

3. Add kale, stir to coat. Cook until kale begins to soften, approximately 5 minutes.

4. Add garlic, salt, and pepper. Cook 1 minute.

5. Remove from heat. Stir in feta crumbles.

6. Spread kale and feta mixture on top of each slice of toast. Slice and enjoy!

7. If adding in eggs, crumbled chicken, or thin-sliced meat, place on top of toast.

The Mom-Lette

The "Mom-Lette"

Eggs provide an easy source of protein, energy, and essential nutrients while the variety of vegetables add taste, texture, fiber, and key nutrients like iron, vitamins A, C, and E, and a good balance of carbohydrates. This recipe can be easily converted to a scrambled egg dish or even baked like a casserole. This recipe can also be used as an easy dinner or cooked in advance and reheated in the morning. Pair it with a slice of toasted multigrain bread or slices of fresh fruit to round out this perfect meal.

Makes 4 to 5 servings

- 1 teaspoon olive oil or light vegetable oil
- 1 tablespoon chopped onion or shallots
- ¼ cup sliced mushrooms
- ½ cup broccoli florets
- ½ cup loosely packed fresh spinach
- ½ cup chopped asparagus
- 2 eggs, beaten
- 1 tablespoon water
- Salt & pepper to taste
- 1 tablespoon shredded cheddar or Swiss cheese (optional)

1. In an 8-inch nonstick skillet, heat oil over medium-high heat. Add onion and mushrooms and cook 2 to 4 minutes, until tender.

2. Add in broccoli florets and cook an additional 4 to 6 minutes. Toss in spinach and cook until spinach wilts, about 2 minutes.

3. Add in asparagus and cook until bright green, about 1 to 2 minutes. Remove vegetables from skillet and keep warm.

4. Combine eggs, water, salt, and pepper in a bowl. Whisk until well mixed.

5. Heat the same 8-inch nonstick skillet used to cook the vegetables over medium-high heat. Quickly pour in the egg mixture.

6. Spread the egg mixture over the bottom of the skillet with a wooden spoon or heat-proof spatula. Let the egg mixture cook 1 to 2 minutes to lightly brown the bottom of the omelet. It should become firm but do not overcook!

7. Spoon the vegetable mixture over half of the omelet.Top with cheese, if using.

8. With the spatula or a spoon, fold the opposite half of the omelet over the vegetables. Cook an additional minute.

9. Gently slide the omelet out of the pan onto a plate and enjoy!

Overnight Oats

Overnight Oats

Oats are a great source of nutrition. They provide fiber to help keep a woman or her family feeling full throughout the morning, and the fiber helps keep the gastrointestinal tract and colon in balance. By replacing sugar with more natural ingredients, these oats will fight off hunger for hours. This recipe can be doubled to make more servings. Plus, they can be prepared the night before and they're ready in the morning to grab and go.

Makes 2 servings

- ½ cup unsweetened almond milk (or skim milk)
- ¾ tablespoon chia seeds
- 2 tablespoons peanut butter (or almond butter), creamy or crunchy
- 1 tablespoon maple syrup or honey
- ½ cup rolled oats (not the quick-cooking kind)
- Optional toppings: granola, more honey, flax seeds, raisins, toasted pumpkin seeds

1. In a small bowl, Mason jar, or 2-cup size measuring cup, add almond milk, chia seeds, peanut butter, and maple syrup (or honey) and stir to combine. (It's OK if the peanut butter isn't completely incorporated or if streaks of peanut butter show.)

2. Add in oats and stir.Make sure all oats are covered with liquid.

3. Cover and refrigerate overnight, or at least 6 hours.

4. Garnish with any desired toppings.

These oats can be kept in the refrigerator for up to 2 days but are best if eaten within 12 to 24 hours of preparation.

Note: The peanut butter can be omitted if someone has a nut allergy.

Perfect Breakfast Burritos

Perfect Breakfast Burritos

This is not your traditional "bacon and eggs" breakfast. Instead, different flavors meld together beautifully into a delicious meal ideal for breakfast, brunch, lunch, or even dinner. Plus, make one batch and you have enough burritos for additional meals or to share with your family. These are so versatile that adding chicken, avocado, sliced beef, or additional vegetables will only enhance the taste. The high protein, fiber, and vitamins in these burritos will give you energy and curb your hunger for hours.

Makes 6 servings

- 3 medium sweet potatoes
- 6 large egg whites
- Vegetable oil or nonstick cooking spray
- 6 large tortillas (whole wheat, spinach, or tomato are best, but any can be used)
- 1 15-ounce can black beans, rinsed and drained
- ¼ teaspoon cumin
- ½ cup low-fat shredded Colby, Swiss, or Monterey Jack cheese
- ⅓ cup mild salsa
- ¼ teaspoon salt
- ⅛ teaspoon black pepper

1. Prepare the sweet potatoes: Stab each sweet potatoes all around several times with a fork. Place in a microwave and cook on high 4 to 6 minutes or until cooked through. (Or, cook in a 400° oven for 40 to 45 minutes.) Once cooked and slightly cooled, remove the skin and place the pulp in a medium bowl. Mash with a fork. Set aside.

2. In a second bowl, beat the egg whites.

3. Spray a medium skillet (preferably nonstick) with vegetable oil or

nonstick cooking spray. Heat pan over medium heat. Add the egg whites and cook, folding occasionally until fluffy. Remove from heat and keep warm.

4. Assemble the Burrito: Warm the tortillas to make them easier to roll. Spread the mashed sweet potatoes on each tortilla.

5. Put eggs, black beans, a sprinkle of cumin, shredded cheese, and a dollop of salsa on each tortilla, leaving about an inch on all sides free. Season with salt and pepper.

6. Tuck in the end and fold the sides. Roll up the burrito and seal the end.

7. Serve with additional salsa or Greek yogurt.

Pumpkin Scones

Pumpkin Scones

Pumpkin is not just a flavor to save only for the fall season or the autumn holidays. In fact, pumpkin is a completely versatile flavor that works well in both sweet and savory dishes. Using a food processor cuts the prep down by more than half and the dough is so well mixed it only needs to be kneaded for a few minutes. These scones contain oats and fiber from the pumpkin, whole-wheat flour, or whatever add-ins you choose. They are low in sugar and use less butter than a traditional scone recipe.

Makes 6-8 scones

- Vegetable spray
- ½ cup pumpkin purée (not pumpkin pie mix—use the plain, unseasoned pumpkin purée)
- 2 tablespoons buttermilk (or regular milk)
- 1 large egg yolk
- ¼ cup old-fashioned rolled oats (not the quick-cook kind)
- 2 cups all-purpose flour
- ½ cup packed light brown sugar
- 1½ teaspoons baking powder (increase it to 2 or 2 ½ teaspoons for more fluffier scones)
- ½ teaspoon baking soda
- ½ teaspoon salt
- 1 tablespoon pumpkin pie spice
- 6 tablespoons cold unsalted butter, cut into cubes
- Optional add-ins: ½ cup(or more depending on taste or preference) dried cranberries, golden raisins, currants, chopped walnuts, dried cherries, or toasted pumpkin seeds
- Optional sprinkle: 1½ teaspoons turbinado sugar

1. Preheat oven to 400°.

2. Line a 9-inch baking pan with parchment paper and spray lightly with vegetable spray.

3. Whisk pumpkin purée, buttermilk, and egg yolk in a small bowl until smooth. Set aside.

4. In a food processor, pulse oats until they resemble coarse meal or sand.

5. Add flour, light brown sugar, baking powder, baking soda, salt, and pumpkin pie spice to oat mix in food processor and pulse until combined.

6. Add butter and pulse until the mix looks like fine sand or coarse meal.

7. If using, add in berries, raisins, seeds, sugar, or any combination and pulse 1 to 2 times to quickly combine.

8. Add pumpkin mix and pulse 3 to 4 times until mix is moistened.

9. Turn dough out onto lightly floured surface and knead gently (about 5 to 6 times) until combined.

10. Press the dough into the prepared pan (it may not all fit but that's OK). It might just be 6 or 7 inches across and about ¾ inch thick. If using, sprinkle the top with the turbinado sugar.

11. Bake 25 to 30 minutes, until the top is golden or begins to crack. Remove from oven and cool 10 to 15 minutes then tip out onto a cutting board. Slice into 8 square or triangular scones. Cool completely.

Quinoa Breakfast Bowl

Quinoa Breakfast Bowl

Quinoa is the perfect ingredient for breakfast. It's naturally high in plant protein and antioxidants. The complex carbohydrates and fiber provide energy for your day and keep you feeling full longer. Quinoa has great texture and a smooth finish. It can be eaten warm or cold, and it reheats easily. The taste can be changed easily by adding any combination of toppings.

Makes 2 servings

- ¾ cup dry quinoa
- 1½ cup water
- ½ cup coconut milk (light coconut milk or almond milk work also)
- ½ cup milk (2%, low fat, or whole)
- 1 tablespoon honey or maple syrup
- 1½ teaspoon cinnamon
- 1½ teaspoon vanilla extract
- Pinch salt
- Optional add-ins: ½ cup raisins (golden or brown), dried cranberries, dried currants
- Optional toppings: fresh blueberries, sliced banana, toasted almonds, pumpkin seeds, chopped peanuts, 1 tablespoon peanut butter, toasted coconut flakes, chia seeds, mini chocolate chips

1. In a medium saucepan, add quinoa and water. Bring to a boil over high heat. Reduce heat and cook for 15 minutes, until fluffy (or according to package directions).

2. With the heat on low, stir in coconut milk, milk, honey or syrup, cinnamon, vanilla, and salt. Cook until the quinoa has absorbed most of the liquid but isn't dry or stiff, about 5 to 7 minutes. If the quinoa becomes too dry, add more milk as needed. Stir in any add-ins, if using.

3. Pour into a bowl, top with any choice or combination of toppings, if using, and enjoy!

Swiss Muesli

Swiss Muesli

Muesli is energy-dense with complex antioxidants. It typically provides 2 to 6 grams of fiber from the whole oats or dried fruits typically mixed with it. There is little to no oil and little, if any, sugar. The flavor of muesli is easy to vary by, for example, toasting the oats prior to adding liquid, using different kinds of milk (e.g., soy, whole, coconut, almond) or yogurts, or adding fresh or dried fruits or nuts. There are also numerous toppings to add on, like granola, honey, fresh maple syrup, agave, turbinado sugar, or toasted pumpkin seeds.

Makes 2 servings

- 2 cups rolled oats (old-fashioned, not instant or steel cut)
- 1 apple chopped
- 1 cup almond, soy, 2%, or nonfat milk
- 1 cup nonfat plain yogurt
- 1 banana, sliced
- 1/4 cup raisins, currants, or dried cranberries
- 1/4 cup chopped walnuts
- 2 tablespoons sliced almonds
- 1 tablespoon brown sugar
- 1 tablespoon honey

1. Mix oats, apple, milk, yogurt, banana, raisins, nuts, brown sugar, and honey together in a bowl.

2. Chill or refrigerate for at least one hour—the longer the muesli chills, the richer the flavors become.

3. Serve cold with a warm cup of herbal tea, warmed milk, or decaffeinated coffee.

For warm muesli: Heat the milk over low heat or slowly in a microwave. Add the warmed milk instead of cold milk and allow the mixture to sit, covered, for up to one hour. Do not refrigerate.

Toasted Muesli with Almonds, Coconut & Dark Chocolate

Makes 2 servings

- 2 cups rolled oats
- 1 cup sliced almonds
- 1 cup unsweetened coconut flakes (or ¼ cup sweetened coconut flakes)
- Pinch salt
- ½ teaspoon cinnamon
- 3 tablespoons maple syrup or honey
- 1 tablespoon light oil (e.g., olive or avocado) or melted unsalted butter
- 2 teaspoons vanilla extract
- ½ cup mini dark chocolate chips
- 1 cup almond, soy, 2%, or nonfat milk
- 1 cup nonfat plain yogurt

1. Preheat oven to 350°. Line a large baking sheet with parchment paper.

2. In a large bowl, combine oats, almonds, coconut, salt, and cinnamon. Mix well.

3. Pour in maple syrup or honey, oil, and vanilla extract. Mix well.

4. Spread oat mix evenly on a baking sheet and bake until the oats and coconut flakes are lightly golden, stirring midway through cooking, 12 to 15 minutes.

5. Allow muesli to cool completely. Mix in chocolate chips when fully cooled.

6. Allow muesli to soak in milk and yogurt for at least one hour.

Store dry, toasted muesli in the freezer for up to two months or in a resealable, airtight container for up to one month in the refrigerator.

Maple Toasted Muesli

Makes 2 servings

- 2 cups rolled oats
- ½ cup sliced almonds
- ¼ cup unsweetened coconut flakes
- ½ teaspoon cinnamon
- ⅛ teaspoon ginger
- ⅛ teaspoon salt
- ⅛ teaspoon nutmeg
- ¼ cup maple syrup
- 1 teaspoon vanilla
- ¼ cup raisins
- 1 cup almond, soy, 2%, or nonfat milk
- 1 cup nonfat plain yogurt

1. Preheat oven to 375°. Line a baking sheet with parchment paper.

2. In a large bowl, combine oats, almonds, coconut flakes, cinnamon, ginger, salt, and nutmeg. Toss together until well mixed.

3. Drizzle in maple syrup and vanilla and stir to combine.

4. Spread oat mix evenly on a baking sheet and bake until the oats and coconut flakes are lightly golden, stirring midway through cooking, 12 to 15 minutes. Remove from oven and cool completely.

5. Add raisins to cooled toasted oat mix and toss to combine.

6. Allow muesli to soak in milk and yogurt for at least one hour.

Store dry, toasted muesli in the freezer for up to two months or in a resealable, airtight container for up to one month in the refrigerator.

Toasted Pumpkin Muesli

Makes 2 servings

- 2 cups rolled oats
- ½ cup raw pumpkin seeds
- ½ cup sliced almonds
- 1 tablespoon unsalted butter, melted
- ½ teaspoon cinnamon
- ¼ teaspoon pumpkin pie spice
- 1 cup almond, soy, 2%, or nonfat milk
- 1 cup nonfat plain yogurt

1. Preheat oven to 350°. Line a baking sheet with parchment paper.

2. In a large bowl, mix oats, pumpkin seeds, almonds, and butter.

3. Spread oat mix evenly on a baking sheet and bake until the oats are lightly golden, stirring midway through cooking, 12 to 15 minutes.

4. Remove from oven and cool slightly. Add in cinnamon and pumpkin pie spice. Stir to combine.

5. Cool completely. Allow muesli to soak in milk and yogurt for at least one hour.

Store dry, toasted muesli in the freezer for up to two months or in a resealable, airtight container for up to one month in the refrigerator.

Gluten-Free Muesli

Makes 2 servings

Bob's Red Mill has an incredible gluten-free muesli mix that is perfect for this recipe. I recommend the entire Bob's Red Mill line of products.

- 2 cups gluten-free rolled oats
- $\frac{1}{2}$ cup sliced almonds
- $\frac{1}{3}$ cup raw pumpkin seeds
- $\frac{1}{3}$ cup dried apricots
- $\frac{1}{3}$ cup dried cherries
- $\frac{1}{3}$ cup raisins
- Pinch salt
- $\frac{1}{2}$ teaspoon cinnamon
- 1 cup almond, soy, 2%, or nonfat milk
- 1 cup nonfat plain yogurt

1. Place the first 8 ingredients in a bowl. Stir to combine.

2. Allow muesli to soak in milk and yogurt for at least one hour. Top with sliced fruit or nuts.

3. Store in an airtight container for 1 to 2 weeks or 1 month in the freezer.

III

Lunch

Black Bean Soup

Black Bean Soup

Black beans are delicious on their own, but they are an amazing addition to salads, pasta dishes, tacos, or egg dishes. Black beans are super healthy, providing protein without sodium, fat, or cholesterol. Contrary to popular myth, beans, especially black beans, are not gas-producing and promote better digestion to leave one feeling fuller longer. This recipe makes a perfect dinner and then additional portions can be reheated easily for lunches or a snack later. This soup also freezes well, so make a batch and save it in individual containers for future meals or a meal on-the-go.

Makes 4 servings

- 2 tablespoons extra-virgin olive oil
- 1 onion, diced
- 2 stalks celery, chopped
- 1 carrot, peeled and chopped
- 2 cloves garlic, minced
- 1 teaspoon salt
- 1 teaspoon freshly ground black pepper
- 1 tablespoon ground cumin
- 4 cans (60 ounces) black beans, drained and rinsed
- 4 cups vegetable stock (or low-sodium chicken broth) (see pages 110 and 111 for homemade stock recipes)
- 1 bay leaf
- Optional: chopped cilantro, toasted pita triangles, chipped avocado, finely diced cashews, a dollop of sour cream, cooked rice, or small dashes of hot sauce

1. In a large stock pot, heat extra-virgin olive oil over medium-high heat. Add onion, celery, and carrot and cook 4 to 5 minutes, until softened.

2. Add garlic, salt, and pepper and cook 8 to 10 minutes, until all vegetables are soft and tender.

3. Add cumin, black beans, vegetable or chicken stock, and bay leaf.

4. Bring to a boil and then reduce to a simmer. Cover pot and cook for 30 minutes, until the black beans are tender.

5. Remove from heat. Remove bay leaf.

6. Insert immersion blender and carefully pulse until soup begins to thicken. Do not over pulse so the soup stays thick.

If no immersion blender is available, carefully ladle 3 to 4 cups of the soup into a blender and purée until smooth. Return to soup and stir until soup is thickened. Repeat until desired thickness is achieved.

7. Spoon into bowls and serve with toppings like chopped cilantro, toasted pita triangles, chipped avocado, finely diced cashews, a dollop of sour cream, cooked rice, or small dashes of hot sauce.

Chicken & Black Bean Quinoa Bowl

Chicken & Black Bean Quinoa Bowl

Quinoa is a great source of protein, fiber, iron, copper, thiamine, vitamin B6, magnesium, phosphorous, and folate. Even better, quinoa has a nutty flavor that complements, or incorporates, into other foods wonderfully. This recipe pairs the taste and benefits of quinoa with black beans and chicken. Black beans are high in protein and fiber. Black beans also require little to no cooking and taste great when added to a dish like this. Chicken adds another layer of flavor and source of protein that keeps this dish versatile for the whole family. The seasonings in this dish are subtle on purpose; pregnant women may have difficulty with the pronounced flavors of cumin and coriander; you can add more, or use less, depending on your own preferences.

Makes 2 servings

- 2 tablespoons extra-virgin olive oil
- 1 garlic clove, minced
- 1 teaspoon paprika
- 1 cup quinoa
- 2 cups water
- 1½ cups diced boneless, skinless chicken breast
- ½ teaspoon cumin
- ½ teaspoon coriander, ground
- ½ teaspoon salt
- ¼ teaspoon fresh ground black pepper
- 2 green onions, sliced (without the white parts)
- 2 plum tomatoes, diced
- 2 cups of canned black beans, rinsed and drained
- 1 cup yellow corn (frozen or fresh)
- ¼ cup chopped cilantro
- 2 tablespoons fresh-squeezed lime juice

1. In a medium saucepan, heat 1 tablespoon extra-virgin olive oil over medium heat. Cook garlic and paprika until fragrant, about 30 seconds to 1 minute.

2. Stir in the quinoa and water. Bring to a boil. Reduce heat, cover, and simmer until no liquid remains, about 12 to 15 minutes.

3. While quinoa is cooking, heat remaining 1 tablespoon of extra-virgin olive oil in a large skillet over medium-high heat. Sauté the chicken, cumin, coriander, salt, and pepper until browned, 5 to 6 minutes.

4. Add green onions, tomatoes, black beans, and corn to the cooked chicken. Cook over medium heat for 4 to 5 minutes, until the onion is softened and the mixture is fragrant.

5. Place cooked quinoa in a bowl. Spoon chicken and black bean mixture over the quinoa. Garnish with cilantro and sprinkle with lime juice.

6. Serve warm or refrigerate in a covered container overnight. Reheat on low heat and stir occasionally during reheating.

Easiest Quiche

Easiest Quiche

This quiche loses the heavy, thick crust of past decades and replaces it with a healthier option, using sweet potatoes. This crust can be varied to use any kind of thinly sliced potato or even cauliflower. The vegetables are sautéed and take on an additional layer of flavor that complements the crust and fluffy eggs. Fontina cheese adds another layer of richness, without a lot of fat, but any soft cheese can used, alone or in combination, to add more depth of flavor. This recipe works well for a lunch, a main course, a midday snack, or for a perfect brunch item.

Makes 8 servings

Crust:

- 1 medium sweet potato
- 1 medium white potato

1. Heat oven to 375°.

2. Spray a 9-inch pie plate with vegetable spray.

3. Using a mandolin, slice the potatoes into thin, ½-inch circles.

4. Layer the potato circles in an overlapping pattern around the bottom of the pie pan and then up the sides. Spray an additional mist of vegetable spray on top of the layered vegetables.

5. Bake for 15 to 20 minutes, until the edges of the potatoes are light brown and slightly crisp. Remove from heat and set aside.

Filling:

- 2 tablespoons extra-virgin olive oil
- 1 green zucchini, sliced into 1/2-inch circles
- 1 yellow squash, sliced into 1/2-inch circles
- 2 carrots, peeled and diced
- 1/2 cup of mushrooms (white, Portobello, or cremini), chopped
- 1 cup broccoli florets
- 2 cloves garlic, minced
- 6 eggs
- 2 egg whites
- 3/4 cup skim milk
- 1 cup Fontina, white cheddar, or mozzarella cheese, grated
- 1/4 cup grated Parmesan cheese

1. Preheat oven to 350°.

2. In a large skillet over medium-high heat, heat the extra-virgin olive oil. Add the zucchini, squash, carrots, mushrooms, and broccoli and sauté until tender, about 5 to 6 minutes.

3. Add garlic and sauté an additional minute. Remove from heat and allow to cool slightly.

4. In a large bowl, beat the eggs and egg whites until combined and fluffy. Add the skim milk and beat until combined and smooth. Add 1 cup of cheese and stir to combine.

5. Pour egg mixture into prepared potato crust, allowing the mix to settle and distribute evenly. Top with Parmesan cheese.

6. Place pie plate on a cooking sheet to capture any spillover. Bake for 35 to 40 minutes, until the egg filling is set and the top is slightly golden. Remove from oven and allow to cool slightly. Slice and serve with a salad, fresh vegetables, mixed fruit, or a slice of toasted multigrain bread.

Fall Soup

Fall Soup

Fall squash is one of the most versatile produce items. It's high in nutrients, easy to cook, and delicious. Roasted squash, like acorn, spaghetti, or butternut, make a great side dish or main course. However, that roasted flavor makes an incredible taste profile for soup. While any squash can be roasted then made into soup, butternut squash has great taste and high amounts of nutrients. Adding in pumpkin gives the soup a creamy texture, a wonderful earthy, seasonal taste, and adds even more fiber, vitamins, and minerals. Using homemade broth elevates this soup to an elegant meal. The recipe can be doubled so it can be frozen in individual containers and thawed for a quick lunch, snack, or dinner.

See homemade broth recipes on pages 110 and 111.

Makes 4-6 servings

- 1-2 butternut squash, peeled, seeded, and cut into 1-inch cubes
- 2-4 tablespoons olive oil (plain or extra-virgin, depending on your preference), plus extra for roasting
- Salt & pepper to taste
- 2 onions, diced
- 1 15-ounce can of pumpkin purée (Do not use pumpkin pie mix! Choose plain pumpkin purée.)
- 4 cups of broth (Chicken or vegetable. If using store bought, choose a low-sodium version.) Homemade broth recipes on pages 110 and 111.

1. Preheat oven to 400°.

2. Toss butternut squash cubes with 1-2 tablespoons of olive oil, salt, and pepper.

3. Spread squash on a parchment paper-lined baking sheet and roast for 20

to 25 minutes. Remove from oven and allow to cool.

4. In a large stock pot or Dutch oven, sauté onions in 1-2 tablespoons of oil. Cook until onions are translucent, about 5-8 minutes.

5. Using a slotted spoon, add in the roasted cubes of butternut squash. Add in the can of pumpkin purée.

6. Add in the broth and stir to combine.

7. Heat until the soup is bubbling. Turn the heat to low and continue cooking until squash is tender and the soup thickens, about 15 to 20 minutes.

8. Purée the soup with an immersion blender, a blender, or a food processor.

Note: If using a blender or food processor, pulse in batches and pour into another bowl.

Once all the soup has been blended or processed, return to the pot and heat through.

9. Sprinkle with toasted croutons and enjoy!

Homemade Broth

Chicken Broth

Makes 4 quarts

- 1-3 pounds of chicken parts (use wings, legs, bones, or chunks of breast or thigh meat)

- 1 onion, cut in quarters
- 4 carrots, peeled and cut into large pieces
- 4 stalks of celery, cut into large pieces (it's OK to leave the leaves attached)
- 4 cloves of garlic, peeled
- Sprigs of thyme and parsley, bundled
- 4 quarts of water

1. Combine all ingredients in a large stock pot.

2. Bring ingredients to a boil over high heat. Turn heat down and simmer for 2 hours.

3. Strain the broth and discard all the meat, vegetables and herbs. Do not add salt.

4. Allow broth to cool. Skim fat off the surface. Freeze in individual containers or refrigerate up to 1 week.

Tip: Both chicken and vegetable broth can be made in a slow cooker or Crock-Pot. Combine all the ingredients in the Crock-Pot or slow cooker and cook on high for 3 hours or low for 5 hours.

Vegetable Broth (this recipe does not contain or use strong acid flavors)

Makes 4 to 6 servings

- 4 stalks of celery, cut into large pieces (it's OK to leave the leaves attached)
- 4 carrots, peeled and cut into large piece
- 2 parsnips, peeled and cut into large pieces

- 2 sweet potatoes, peeled and cut into large chunks or quarters
- 4 cloves of garlic, peeled
- 3 onions, cut into quarters
- 4-6 cups of water

1. Combine all ingredients in a large stock pot.

2. Bring to a boil over high heat.

3. Reduce heat to medium and simmer for about 30- 45 minutes or until vegetables are all softened.

4. Strain broth and allow to cool.

5. Store in individual containers and freeze. Or refrigerate for up to 1 week.

Tip: Both chicken and vegetable broth can be made in a slow cooker or Crock-Pot. Combine all the ingredients in the Crock-Pot or slow cooker and cook on high for 3 hours or low for 5 hours.

Greek Meatball Salad

Greek Meatball Salad

This salad is high in protein and flavor. You can make the meatballs in advance and then add them to the salad base. The salad can be any combination of greens you prefer—the meatballs pair well with almost any combination of vegetables. The dressing is easy to prepare, stores well in the refrigerator, and can be easily stored in its own container then poured over the salad right before eating to keep the greens or vegetables crisp and the meatballs tender. This salad can also serve as a simple dinner, especially during summer, or as the perfect dish to bring to a party, to a backyard barbeque, to a beach house, on a boat ride, or on a camping trip. Any of the ingredients can be modified according to your tastes and can be doubled or tripled, depending on the number of people. Serve this alongside crusty bread, pita triangles, fresh fruit, or olives.

Makes 2 to 4 servings

Tzatziki Sauce

- 1 cucumber
- ½ teaspoon salt
- 2 cups nonfat Greek yogurt
- 1½ tablespoon fresh lemon juice
- 1 tablespoon extra-virgin olive oil
- 1 garlic clove, minced
- 1 tablespoon chopped fresh dill
- Pinch fresh black pepper

Meatballs

- ¾ cup cooked couscous, cooled
- 1 egg, lightly beaten
- 1 tablespoon chopped fresh mint

- 2 cloves garlic, minced
- Pinch of salt
- Pinch of fresh ground black pepper
- ½ pound ground beef
- ½ ground lamb (or use pork, depending on preference)
- 1½ tablespoons extra-virgin olive oil

Salad

- 5 to 6 cups chopped lettuce (Romaine or Iceberg)
- 1 cucumber, peeled and cut into one-inch chunks
- 1 cup grape or cherry tomatoes, whole or chopped
- ½ cup carrots, chopped
- ½ cup celery, chopped
- ½ cup watermelon, cubed
- ½ cup black olives, chopped

Prepare the sauce:

1. Peel the cucumber and remove the seeds. Grate onto a dishtowel, washcloth, or cheesecloth. Roll into a ball and squeeze out the liquid. Place in a strainer and drain any remaining liquid.

2. Sprinkle salt over the cucumber and toss to coat. Allow to drain 30 to 40 minutes. Squeeze out remaining liquid once more.

3. Add all remaining ingredients and stir to combine. Set aside.

Prepare the meatballs:

1. Preheat oven to 350°.

2. Combine the couscous, egg, mint, garlic, salt and pepper in a large bowl.

3. Add beef and lamb and mix well.

4. Shape into 12 to 14 meatballs.

5. Heat extra-virgin olive oil in a large skillet over medium heat. Brown half the meatballs in the oil on all sides until evenly browned. Transfer to a baking sheet lined with paper towels to drain. Brown the remaining half of meatballs.

6. Bake meatballs until cooked through, 15 to 17 minutes.

7. Allow to cool slightly.

Prepare salad:

1. Toss lettuce, cucumbers, tomatoes, carrots, celery, watermelon and black olives.

2. Add meatballs and top with tzatziki sauce.

Pumpkin Soup

Pumpkin Soup

This soup is velvety smooth, perfect as comfort food on a chilly day, and stores well in the refrigerator. It incorporates coconut milk for extra richness without the burden of lactose, and it can be made as thick or thin as you like. Different toppings easily change the texture of this soup. This soup provides protein and about 4 to 8 grams of fiber, so it's healthy, delicious, and easy!

Makes 4 to 6 servings

- 1 tablespoon extra-virgin olive oil
- 2 medium shallots, diced
- 2 cloves garlic, minced
- 2½ cups purée pumpkin (either roasted fresh or from a quality canned brand. Do not use pumpkin pie mix—be careful and ensure the label says pure pumpkin purée.)
- 1 cup light coconut milk (or light cream)
- 2 tablespoons Grade A maple syrup or honey
- ¼ teaspoon salt
- ¼ teaspoon fresh ground black pepper
- ¼ teaspoon cinnamon
- ¼ teaspoon nutmeg
- Toppings: toasted pumpkin seeds, almonds, sesame seeds, or a dollop of crème fraiche or cream

1. In a large saucepan over medium heat, add extra-virgin olive oil and sauté shallots and garlic, 2 to 3 minutes, until slightly browned and translucent.

2. Add all remaining ingredients and bring to a simmer.

3. Once simmering, use an immersion blender or conventional blender to purée soup to desired consistency.

4. Continue to cook over medium-low heat for 5 to 10 minutes. Adjust seasonings to taste as needed.

5. Serve warm. Top with toasted pumpkin seeds, almonds, sesame seeds, or a dollop of crème fraiche or cream.

"Souper" Soups

"Souper" Soups

This soup starts with a "base" and then different variations can be made from the simple base recipe. Soups can be made in small batches and take only a short time to make. These recipes can be doubled and tripled. Pair these soups with toasted bread or pita pieces, unsalted crackers, or top them with different flavors, like a sprinkle of toasted pumpkin or sesame seeds, croutons, a drizzle of extra-virgin olive oil or pesto, or a light shaving of cheese.

Basic Soup Recipe

Serves 4 to 6

- 2 tablespoons extra-virgin olive oil
- 2 carrots, peeled and diced
- 2 celery stalks, diced
- 1 medium yellow onion, diced
- 2 garlic cloves, minced
- 1 teaspoon dried oregano
- 1 teaspoon dried basil
- 8 cups water or stock (chicken, vegetable, or beef)

1. Heat oil in a large stock pot of Dutch oven over medium-high heat.

2. Sauté vegetables until onions are soft and translucent, about 6 to 8 minutes. Add the seasonings.

3. Add in water or stock and bring to a boil. Reduce heat to low-medium and simmer covered for 20 to 30 minutes, until vegetables have softened.

Lentil Soup

Makes 4 servings

Basic Soup Recipe above but add to the sautéed vegetables:

- 1 bay leaf
- 2 cups dried lentils (green, red, or yellow)
- 1 14.5-ounce can crushed tomatoes
- Salt & pepper to taste
- Optional: 1 cup roughly chopped Swiss chard, escarole, spinach and ½ teaspoon balsamic vinegar

1. Bring the Basic Soup recipe with the additional 3 ingredients to a boil over medium-high heat.

2. Reduce heat and simmer over medium heat 60 to 90 minutes, until lentils soften.

3. If using, add chard, escarole,or spinach and vinegar immediately before serving. Season with salt and pepper to taste.

Chicken & Pasta Soup

Makes 4 servings

Basic Soup Recipe above but add to the sautéed vegetables:

- 5 cups water or stock (chicken or vegetable)
- 1 bay leaf
- 1 teaspoon thyme
- 1 pound boneless chicken breast, cooked and cut into 1-inch pieces or shredded

- 1 12-ounce package of elbow-shaped pasta, cooked and drained
- 1 bunch kale, shredded

1. Make Basic Soup Recipe above but add to the sautéed vegetables the water or broth, bay leaf, and thyme. Bring to a boil then reduce heat to medium and simmer 15 minutes.

2. Add chicken, pasta, and kale and simmer an additional 10 to 12 minutes, until kale is softened.

Vegetable Soup

Makes 4 servings

Basic Soup Recipe plus:

- 1 14-ounce can diced tomatoes, in their liquid
- 2 medium potatoes, peeled and diced into 1-inch cubes
- 1 bay leaf
- ½ teaspoon dried thyme
- 1 cup frozen green peas
- 1 cup frozen yellow corn
- 1 cup frozen green beans
- ½ cup chopped parsley
- Salt & pepper to taste

1. Add tomatoes, potatoes, and bay leaf to sautéed vegetables in Basic Soup Recipe. Bring to a boil over medium-high heat. Add the green peas, yellow corn, and green beans and reduce heat to medium. Simmer for 20 to 30 minutes.

2. Add peas, corn, and parsley and cook an additional 5 minutes.

3. Season with salt and pepper before serving. Garnish with additional parsley when serving.

Spinach & Egg Casserole

Spinach & Egg Casserole

This spinach and egg casserole covers all the necessary bases. It's made with eggs so it can be a breakfast dish or for dinner. It's packed with vegetables so it has the right amount of fiber. It's not sweet but can be made more savory by adding additional seasonings, like garlic or cumin, depending on how you like your vegetables. Even better, it can be made ahead of time and reheated when it's brunch time or divided into portions and reheated individually. Prep time is quick, and you can customize this any way you wish by adding different vegetables, bacon, leftover chicken, cheeses, or herbs.

Makes 6 to 8 servings

- 1 tablespoon extra-virgin olive oil
- 1 cup sliced mushrooms
- ½ chopped onion
- 1 cup chopped tomato (seeds and pulp removed)
- 2 to 3 cups spinach (1 package fresh or 2 boxes frozen spinach thawed and squeezed dry)
- 1¼ cups shredded cheddar (mild or sharp)
- 2 whole eggs
- 2 egg whites
- Salt & pepper to taste
- Optional: 3 slices of bacon, cooked and crumbled

1. Preheat oven to 375°. Spray an 8x8-inch or 9-inch round pan with vegetable spray or brush with olive oil.

2. In a medium skillet over medium-high heat, heat olive oil. Add in mushrooms and onion and sauté 6 to 8 minutes or until onions are translucent and mushrooms are soft. Add in diced tomatoes and cook an additional minute.

3. Place half the sautéed vegetables in the bottom of the baking dish. Add half the spinach on top of vegetables. Alternate layers of vegetables and spinach.

4. Whisk eggs and egg whites until fluffy. Season with salt and pepper. Pour over the vegetable and spinach mixture.

5. Sprinkle bacon (if using) across the top.

6. Sprinkle cheese over the top.

7. Bake uncovered for 35 to 40 minutes. Remove from oven and allow to cool and set, 15 to 20 minutes.

8. Cut and serve in squares.

Thai Chicken & Zucchini Noodle Salad

Thai Chicken & Zucchini Noodle Salad

The zucchini "noodles" in this dish add a great texture and incredible flavor. This dish is so easy and is perfect for lunch or for a summer dinner when it's too hot to cook. Using rotisserie or leftover chicken cuts down the prep time, and the vegetables in this dish add fiber, flavor, and texture. Any of the seasonings can be adjusted according to taste—or make you own combination of flavors and experiment. The zucchini noodles can hold up to sauces and seasonings and don't wilt or get soggy quickly. They also hold up in the refrigerator and you can make the vinaigrette in advance and set it aside to add on your salad right before you're ready to eat. You can also swap out the chicken for tuna, salmon, or leftover beef or pork.

Vinaigrette

- 2½ tablespoons rice wine vinegar
- 1 tablespoon sesame oil
- 2 teaspoons honey
- 1 teaspoon fresh-squeezed lime juice
- 1 garlic clove, minced
- 1 green onion, finely chopped
- 1 tablespoon sesame seeds
- Salt & pepper to taste

Salad

- 3 green zucchini, "spiralized" into noodles, food processed or grated into shreds
- 1 cooked chicken breast (poached, baked, grilled, or rotisserie), shredded
- 2 Roma tomatoes, seeded and diced
- 2 carrots, shredded
- ½ cup green onions, diced

- 1 cup shelled edamame
- 1 cup kale, shredded
- 1 cup Napa or red cabbage, shredded

Garnish

- Chopped fresh cilantro, chopped peanuts, chopped walnuts, toasted pumpkin seeds, toasted sesame seeds, pomegranate seeds, fresh sprouts

Prepare the vinaigrette:

1. In a small bowl, whisk the rice wine vinegar, sesame oil, honey, lime juice, garlic, green onion, sesame seeds, salt, and pepper until combined. Set aside.

Prepare the salad:

1. In a large bowl, add the zucchini noodles, chicken, tomatoes, carrots, green onions, edamame, kale, and cabbage. Toss to combine.

2. Drizzle some of the vinaigrette over the salad and toss again to coat.

3. Garnish with cilantro, nuts, seeds, or sprouts.

If making in advance, prepare the salad and store in a closed container. Store the vinaigrette separately. Drizzle the vinaigrette over the salad immediately before serving.

Tomato & Avocado Burgers

Tomato & Avocado Burgers

This recipe is **so** simple and packed with great, flavorful ingredients. This recipe can be customized to taste easily. It's gluten-free, high in protein, and low in carbohydrates to keep feeling full longer.

Makes 2 servings

- 2 large beefsteak tomatoes
- 1 ripe avocado, divided
- 2 tablespoons plain Greek yogurt
- 1 tablespoon mayonnaise
- 2 teaspoons fresh lime juice
- ¼ teaspoon ground cumin
- ½ pound of ground turkey
- ¼ teaspoon salt
- ½ teaspoon pepper
- Vegetable spray or olive oil
- Large pinch of fresh sprouts, julienned basil, or spinach (any fresh green works)

1. Slice tomatoes in half. Using a spoon, scoop out tomato seeds and pulp. Set aside.

2. Place half avocado in a bowl and mash with a fork until smooth. Add yogurt, mayonnaise, lime juice, and cumin. Stir to combine.

3. Dice remaining half of avocado and add to mix with salt. Stir gently to combine and set aside.

4. Season turkey with ¼ teaspoon of salt and ½ teaspoon of pepper. Mix well.

5. Divide turkey mix into two. Form 2 patties approximately ½ inch thick.

6. Heat a grill pan, skillet, or outdoor grill over medium-high heat. Grill turkey patties 2 to 3 minutes on each side until cooked. Set aside.

7. Lightly spray a skillet or brush with olive oil. Cook tomato halves, open side down, 2 to 3 minutes, until they begin to brown. Flip and cook the outside for 20 to 30 seconds to color the skin.

8. Assemble the burgers: place a large pinch of greens on the bottom part of the tomatoes. Top with a turkey patty, 1 to 2 tablespoons of avocado sauce, and tomato top

Turkey Pesto Roll Ups

Turkey Pesto Roll Ups

Turkey is a great source of protein and can be fresh roasted, leftover, or the low-sodium store-bought kind. The spinach adds some fiber, iron, and texture. Wraps, or tortilla bread, come in a variety of flavors to provide a nice boost of energy-producing carbohydrates. The cheese adds additional protein and calcium.

Makes 2 to 4 servings

- 2 whole-wheat tortillas (or any flavor or gluten-free)
- 4 teaspoons of pesto (homemade or store bought)
- 2 ounces of sliced, roasted turkey breast (approximately 3 to 4 slices)
- 1 tablespoon shredded mozzarella cheese (or 2 thin slices of Provolone cheese)
- 1 cup baby spinach leaves

1. Spread 2 teaspoons of pesto over each tortilla, leaving about an inch uncovered around the edge.

2. Evenly layer on the turkey, mozzarella, and spinach leaves (about 10 to 12 leaves, or ½cup per tortilla).

3. Fold in the sides and roll the tortilla. Place it seam side down.

Optional: The tortilla can be microwaved on a microwave-safe plate for 20 to 25 seconds on medium heat or placed in a Panini press for 1 to 2 minutes, until slightly browned.

4. Slice each wrap into 2 halves and serve with a tossed green salad.

IV

Dinner

Angels' Ears Pasta

Angels' Ears Pasta

This recipe gets its name from the orecchiette pasta—small shell-shaped pasta that looks like a tiny ear, or the ear of an angel. It provides a good serving of vegetables from the broccoli which, when mixed with the seasoning and added to the hot pasta, becomes a delicious broccoli pesto. This recipe is a great time saver because the pasta and the broccoli cook together. By using chicken sausage, there are less fat and spices than traditional pork sausage. The pasta can be any kind or shape of pasta, including gluten-free or whole wheat. Using fresh-grated cheese adds a velvety finish.

Makes 6 to 8 servings

- 12-14 ounces chicken sausage, casing removed, crumbled
- 1 cup uncooked orecchiette pasta
- 6 cups fresh broccoli florets, no stems, or 16 ounces frozen broccoli florets
- 2 tablespoons extra-virgin olive oil, divided
- 1 small yellow onion, diced
- 4 cloves garlic, chopped
- ¼ cup fresh-grated Romano cheese or fresh-grated Parmigiano-Reggiano cheese
- Salt & pepper to taste

1. Bring 5 quarts of water to a boil.

2. In a large nonstick skillet over medium-high heat, brown sausage until cooked, about 5 to 8 minutes. Remove from heat and drain cooked sausage crumbles on paper towels.

3. Add pasta to the boiling water and return to a boil. Add broccoli and cook according to the pasta directions until al dente.

4. When pasta is done, reserve 1 cup of the pasta liquid and set aside. Drain the pasta and the broccoli.

5. Return the pasta pot to the stove. Add 1 tablespoon of the extra-virgin olive oil and heat over high heat.

6. Add the onion and cook 4 to 5 minutes, until softened.

7. Add the garlic and cook 1 minute.

8. Reduce heat and add the pasta and broccoli back to the pot. Add in the sausage.

9. Mix well. Add in the remaining tablespoon of extra-virgin olive oil, grated cheese, salt, and pepper.

10. Add in ½ cup of the reserved pasta water and mix well. Add more of the reserved pasta water until the sauce is of the desired consistency.

11. Serve in bowls and top with additional grated cheese, chopped parsley or basil, or a small squeeze of lemon juice.

Apple Glazed Chicken

Apple Glazed Chicken

The flavors of the garlic, mustard, and apple cider combine to make a delicious sauce for the chicken (or any meat!). The addition of apples adds another layer of texture and flavor. You can change up the vegetables and add in potatoes, cabbage, Swiss chard, broccolini, escarole, or even kale and make this an even heartier meal. Pair this with fresh bread or toasted pita triangles or slices of rye, sourdough, pumpernickel, or gluten-free bread.

Makes 4 servings

- 2 tablespoons extra-virgin olive oil
- 4 skinless, boneless chicken breast halves (4 to 6 ounces each)
- ¼ teaspoon salt
- ½ teaspoon black pepper
- 1 garlic clove, minced
- 2 tablespoons Dijon mustard or Spicy Brown mustard
- 1 cup apple cider
- 2 medium Granny Smith or McIntosh apples, cored and sliced (OK to peel in advance if preferred)
- 6 cups fresh spinach

1. Heat extra-virgin olive oil in a large skillet over medium-high heat.

2. Pat chicken dry with paper towels. Sprinkle both sides with salt and pepper. Add to heated skillet and cook until browned, about 5 to 7 minutes per side. Remove chicken to a plate and keep warm. Save juices.

3. Add garlic, mustard, apple cider, and apple slices to the skillet and bring to a boil. Reduce heat and simmer, stirring often, 5 to 8 minutes, until apples are slightly softened.

4. Return the chicken and any juices to the skillet. Cook, stirring occasion-

ally, until the chicken is cooked through and sauce thickens, about 2 to 3 minutes.

5. Add spinach to the skillet in small batches and toss until wilted, about 1 to 2 minutes.

6. Serve hot; drizzle with any additional sauce from the skillet.

Beef & Broccoli

Beef & Broccoli

Beef and broccoli is a traditional Chinese dish that can be healthy if the right cuts of meat are used and the sauce is made fresh. This beef and broccoli recipe is lower in sodium, full of fiber, thanks to the broccoli, and lower in fat. This recipe uses cornstarch to build a thicker sauce, instead of MSG (monosodium glutamate), and low-sodium soy sauce available in most grocery stores. Brown rice adds extra fiber and flavor.

Makes 2 to 4 servings

Coating

- 2 tablespoons cornstarch
- 2 tablespoons water
- ½ teaspoon garlic powder

Meat

- 1 pound boneless chuck steak, cut into thin strips
- 1 tablespoon vegetable oil
- *Vegetables:*
- 1 tablespoon vegetable oil
- 4 cups broccoli florets
- 1 small onion, sliced

Sauce

- ⅓ cup low-sodium soy sauce
- 1½ tablespoons brown sugar
- 1 teaspoon ground ginger
- 1 tablespoon cornstarch
- 1 tablespoon cold water

Rice

- 2 cups cooked brown rice

1. Prepare the coating: In a small bowl, combine cornstarch, water, and garlic powder until smooth.

2. Add the beef strips to the coating mixture. Toss to coat.

3. In a large skillet (or wok) over medium-high heat, add 1 tablespoon vegetable oil and stir fry the beef until cooked, 4 to 5 minutes. Remove and keep warm.

4. In the same skillet, add 1 tablespoon of vegetable oil and stir fry the broccoli and onion until cooked, 4 to 5 minutes.

5. Return the beef to the skillet.

6. Prepare the sauce. Combine the soy sauce, brown sugar, ginger, cornstarch, and water until smooth. Add to the skillet.

7. Cook and stir beef and broccoli in sauce 2 to 3 minutes.

8. Serve over brown rice.

Note: Use any leftover rice and make Rice Pudding!

Beef Enchiladas

Beef Enchiladas

This dish can be made as bland or spicy as you wish. The addition of salsa provides extra flavor and fiber. Homemade salsa is so easy to make and keeps very well in the refrigerator to use on leftovers, for snacks, or on top of chicken, pork, beef, or even tofu for another night's meal.

Makes 6 servings

- 1 pound extra lean ground beef (or chicken or turkey)
- 1 medium yellow onion, chopped
- 2 garlic cloves, minced
- 1 teaspoon ground cumin
- ½ teaspoon black pepper
- 10 small corn or multigrain tortillas
- 1 10-ounce can of red enchilada sauce (or tomato sauce)
- 1 cup shredded light yellow cheddar cheese
- Optional toppings or garnish: sliced black olives, chopped cilantro or parsley, or fresh salsa

1. Preheat oven to 350°. Spray a 9x13-inch baking dish with vegetable spray.

2. In a large skillet over medium-high heat, brown the chopped beef and onion, about 5 to 8 minutes, until meat is no longer pink and onion is soft and translucent.

3. Add the garlic, cumin, and black pepper. Cook an additional 3 to 4 minutes, until the garlic is cooked and fragrant. Remove from heat.

4. Stack the tortillas and wrap in a damp paper towel. Microwave on high for 10 to 12 seconds, until the tortillas are warm and softened.

5. Spread some of the red enchilada sauce (or tomato sauce) on the bottom

of the prepared baking dish.

6. Top each tortilla with 2 to 3 tablespoonfuls of the beef mixture. Roll each tortilla and place it seam side down in the baking dish. Repeat with the remaining tortillas.

7. Pour remaining sauce over the rolled enchiladas and spread to cover evenly. Sprinkle with cheddar cheese.

8. Bake uncovered 20 to 25 minutes, until the cheese is browned and bubbly. Remove from oven and allow to cool 5 to 10 minutes. Serve alongside a green salad, yellow rice, or polenta. Garnish with toppings of your choice.

Black Bean Burgers

Black Bean Burgers

Black bean burgers are a delicious alternative to traditional beef burgers. This recipe keeps the burger juicy and not pasty. Unlike frozen black bean burgers, this recipe stays together nicely and can be grilled, baked, or browned easily. The spices and seasonings can be adjusted to make it mild or spicy, and the recipe can be doubled or tripled to make burgers that can be easily frozen and thawed when needed. These burgers can be served with salads, fresh vegetables, or simple side dishes. They can also be crumbled and added to sauces, pastas, or as a protein source in salads.

Makes 6 servings

- 2 14-ounce cans black beans, drained and rinsed and patted dry
- 1 tablespoon extra-virgin olive oil
- 1 cup finely chopped yellow onion
- 2 cloves garlic, minced
- 1 teaspoon ground cumin
- ¼ teaspoon paprika
- ½ teaspoon garlic powder
- ½ cup fresh or dried breadcrumbs, oatmeal, or oat flour
- ½ cup crumbled feta cheese
- 1 egg
- 2 teaspoons Worcestershire sauce
- 2 tablespoons ketchup, steak sauce, mayo or barbeque sauce
- Salt & pepper to taste
- Optional: ½ to 1 teaspoon of chili powder

1. Preheat oven to 325°. Spread beans on a parchment-lined baking sheet and bake 15 minutes, until slightly dry.

2. Heat extra-virgin olive oil in a medium skillet over medium-high heat. Sauté onion and garlic until softened and fragrant, 5 to 6 minutes.

3. In a large bowl, combine sautéed onion and garlic and add all ingredients, except the black beans. Stir to combine.

4. Add in the beans and stir to combine.

5. With a fork or a masher, crush some of the beans so the mixture becomes slightly dense. Do not mash all the beans—leave some whole.

6. Using a ⅓ cup measure, scoop out some of the bean mix. Form into a round patty. Repeat until all the bean mix is used.

7. To cook:

- Grill: Over low flame or on a piece of greased foil, grill black bean burger patties 6 to 8 minutes per side, until browned and cooked through.
- Bake: Preheat oven to 375°. Place black bean burger patties on a foil- or parchment-lined baking sheet lightly sprayed with vegetable spray. Bake 10 minutes per side until slightly browned and cooked through.

Serve on top of a salad, broccoli slaw, lettuce leaves, tomato and avocado slices, sliced cucumbers, or a cucumber salad.

Top with pesto (see my recipe for Perfect Pesto!) or serve on a multigrain roll.

Chicken & Mushrooms

Chicken & Mushrooms

This is an easy dish to make when time is short. It uses simple, healthy ingredients, but it tastes like you cooked it for hours!

Makes 4 to 6 servings

- 2 tablespoons extra-virgin olive oil, divided
- 2 tablespoons butter, divided
- ½ cup diced yellow onion
- 2 cups sliced mushrooms (white, Portobello, or cremini)
- 1 clove garlic, chopped
- ½ cup chicken broth, divided
- ½ cup dry white wine or sherry (optional)
- 1½ pounds skinless, boneless chicken thighs
- ¼ teaspoon salt
- ½ teaspoon fresh ground black pepper
- 1 tablespoon all-purpose flour
- ½ cup chopped parsley
- 2 teaspoons lemon zest

1. Heat 1 tablespoon of extra-virgin olive oil in a large, nonstick skillet over medium-high heat. Melt in 1 tablespoon of butter and add in the onions and mushrooms. Cook for 5 to 6 minutes, until onions are translucent and softened. Add in the garlic and ¼ cup chicken broth and cook an additional 1 minute.

2. Uncover for 4 to 5 minutes, until most of the liquid evaporates. Add wine or sherry, if using, and stir to scrape up any browned bits from the bottom of the pan. Pour mixture into a small bowl and set aside.

3. Pat the chicken thighs dry with a paper towel. Sprinkle with salt and pepper and coat lightly in flour.

4. Heat remaining 1 tablespoon of butter and 1 tablespoon of extra-virgin olive oil in skillet and add chicken. Cook on each side until lightly browned, about 4 minutes per side. Remove from platter, cover with foil, and keep warm.

5. Return mushroom mixture to skillet and add in remaining ¼ cup chicken broth and scrape any remaining brown bits from the bottom of the pan. (Optional: Add in another 1 tablespoon of butter for a smooth, glossy sauce.) Add the chicken and any of its juices back to the pan. Heat through over low heat for 6 to 8 minutes. Sprinkle with parsley and lemon zest.

6. Serve chicken over rice, quinoa, spiralized vegetables, or whole-wheat pasta. Pour mushroom sauce over chicken. Serve alongside steamed broccoli, green beans, asparagus, or a crispy tossed salad, arugula salad, or kale salad.

Chicken & Vegetable Stir Fry

Chicken & Vegetable Stir Fry

This dish has all the dinner essentials: protein, fiber from vegetables, the right amount of seasoning, texture, and, of course, flavor. In addition, this recipe is so easy to create, and you can substitute any meat or vegetable. The base sauce for the stir fry stays the same so feel free to experiment and try different meats or protein sources, vegetables, or add-ins.

Makes 4 servings

- 8 ounces skinless, boneless chicken breast, cut into small (about 1-inch pieces)
- 2 tablespoons low-sodium soy sauce
- 1 teaspoon sesame oil
- 1 tablespoon cornstarch
- 1 tablespoon light vegetable or avocado oil
- 2 cups broccoli florets, cut into pieces
- 1/2 cup chopped asparagus
- 1 medium zucchini cut into small chunks or squares
- 2 carrots, peeled and diced
- 2 cloves garlic, minced
- 1/2 cup chicken or vegetable broth
- 1 tablespoon extra-virgin olive oil
- 1 tablespoon honey
- 1/2 teaspoon fresh-grated ginger
- 3 green onions, finely chopped

1. Combine chicken pieces, soy sauce, sesame oil, and cornstarch in a bowl. Set aside

2. Heat vegetable or avocado oil in a large skillet or wok over medium-high heat. Add broccoli, asparagus, zucchini, carrots, and garlic. Cook, stirring often, 2 to 4 minutes, until tender-crisp.

3. Add chicken or vegetable broth and cover. Simmer until vegetables are tender, about 5 to 6 minutes. Transfer vegetables and sauce into a large bowl and cover to keep warm.

4. Wipe out the skillet or wok. Heat the extra-virgin olive oil in the skillet or wok over medium-high heat. Cook the chicken mixture, stirring occasionally, until chicken is no longer pink, about 4 to 5 minutes.

5. Add in the honey and ginger. Stir in the vegetables. Continue to cook, stirring frequently, 2 to 3 minutes, until sauce thickens.

6. Serve over brown rice, quinoa, or rice noodles. Garnish with a sprinkle of green onion.

Chicken Fajitas

Chicken Fajitas

This recipe is super easy to put together. It can all be done in one skillet and is ready in minutes. When it's all done, it's a low-sodium, high-protein dish that's full of flavor. Change up the chicken to pork, beef, or tofu. Try changing up the vegetables to add in more crunchy vegetables like shredded Brussels sprouts, green beans, sprouts, edamame, or celery.

Makes 4 servings

- 1 pound boneless chicken breasts, sliced in thin strips
- 2 tablespoons fresh parsley (or cilantro)
- 2 tablespoons extra-virgin olive oil, plus 2 teaspoons
- 1 teaspoon dried oregano
- 1/2 teaspoon sweet paprika
- 1/2 teaspoon salt
- 1/4 teaspoon garlic powder
- 2 carrots, peeled and thinly sliced
- 1/2 cup shredded coleslaw mix
- 1/2 yellow onion, thinly sliced
- 1/2 teaspoon chili powder (optional)
- Salt & pepper to taste
- 2 tomatoes, seeded and thinly sliced
- Juice of 1/2 lime

1. In a large bowl, combine chicken, parsley, 1 tablespoon extra-virgin olive oil, oregano, sweet paprika, salt, and garlic powder. Toss until chicken is well coated in the seasoning mix. Refrigerate for at least 30 minutes.

2. Heat 1 tablespoon extra-virgin olive oil in a nonstick skillet over medium-high heat. When the skillet is hot, add carrots, slaw mix, onion, chili powder, if using, and Salt and pepper to taste. Sauté 5 to 6 minutes, until vegetables are softened and slightly browned. Add the tomatoes and cook 2 minutes,

stirring frequently. Remove vegetable mix from the skillet onto a plate and set aside.

3. Slowly add the chicken to the hot skillet and cook 2 to 4 minutes on each side until cooked through and no longer pink.

4. Add the vegetables back into the skillet and add in the lime juice. Stir to combine and cook until heated through.

5. Serve with multigrain wraps, over rice or black beans, in lettuce leaf wraps, or with toasted pita chips. Top with salsa, extra diced tomatoes, or diced scallions.

Chicken Tacos

Chicken Tacos

This recipe uses lean chicken as the main source of protein. This recipe can also be modified with salmon instead of chicken. Dried spices are substituted with natural, fresh flavors. It's low in sodium, fat, and cholesterol and high in protein. This recipe can be doubled or tripled, and leftovers reheat perfectly for lunch or another satisfying dinner.

Makes 4 servings

- 1 pound thin-sliced boneless chicken breast, cut into strips (or use salmon, lean pork, or lean beef)
- 2 limes, juiced and divided
- 1 teaspoon ground cumin, divided
- 1 teaspoon garlic powder, divided
- 1 teaspoon paprika, divided
- 2 Roma or plum tomatoes, diced
- 1 yellow onion, thinly sliced
- 4 multigrain tortillas
- Salt & pepper to taste
- 1 tablespoon chopped fresh cilantro
- Greek yogurt or sour cream

1. Combine chicken, half the lime juice, ½ teaspoon cumin, ½ teaspoon garlic powder, and ½ teaspoon paprika in a bowl. Marinate for 10 to 30 minutes.

2. In a large nonstick skillet over medium-high heat, sauté tomatoes, onion, ½ teaspoon lime juice, ½ teaspoon cumin, ½ teaspoon garlic powder, and ½ teaspoon paprika until onion is tender-crisp, about 5 minutes.

3. In another nonstick skillet, sauté chicken mixture over medium-high heat until chicken is no longer pink, about 5 to 10 minutes.

4. Layer tortillas between slightly moistened paper towels on a microwave-safe plate. Heat until warm, about 10 to 20 seconds.

5. Spoon chicken and vegetable mixture onto tortillas. Top with cilantro, lime juice, and a scoop of Greek yogurt or sour cream onto top. Serve alongside fresh green salad, yellow rice, or a bean salad.

Confetti Shrimp Tacos

Confetti Shrimp Tacos

This recipe is a delicious, colorful combination of both sweet and savory. The shrimp provides protein, while the other ingredients provide fiber, flavor, and texture. It's simple to prepare, and the recipe can be doubled or tripled to make this a family meal, a lunch, or a perfect dish to bring to a party.

Makes 3 to 4 servings

- 4 to 6 ounces medium fresh shrimp, peeled, cleaned, and tails removed
- Salt and pepper to taste
- 1/4 teaspoon sweet paprika (plus one pinch to season shrimp)
- 2 teaspoons extra-virgin olive oil
- 1/2 cup fresh or frozen yellow corn
- 1/2 medium mango, peeled and chopped
- 1/2 cup diced tomato
- 2 ounces feta cheese, crumbled
- 1 tablespoon fresh-squeezed lime juice
- 3 to 4 corn tortillas
- Chopped fresh cilantro, parsley, and basil for garnish

1. Season shrimp on both sides with salt and pepper and a pinch of paprika.

2. In a large nonstick skillet heated over medium-high heat, heat extra-virgin olive oil. Add shrimp and cook 2 minutes per side, until pink and cooked through. Remove from heat and cool slightly. Rough chop when slightly cooled.

3. In a medium bowl, stir chopped shrimp, corn, mango, tomato, feta cheese, and lime juice.

4. Warm the tortillas in a microwave (stack between slightly moistened

paper towels on a microwave-safe plate and heat 30 seconds to 1 minute on high) or warm in a skillet over medium heat, 20 to 30 seconds per side.

5. Build the tacos by spooning shrimp mixture inside or over warm tortillas. Garnish with chopped cilantro, parsley, and basil.

Easy Chicken Piccata

Easy Chicken Piccata

This recipe makes an elegant-looking dinner in under 30 minutes. Chicken piccata is a recipe that anyone can make because the ingredients are basic, and the preparation is easy with only 1 pan. It can be paired with a seasonal vegetable, pasta, or rice. Even better, it reheats beautifully, or it can be taken as lunch the following day or diced up and tossed with greens to make a delicious salad.

Makes 4 servings

- 2 tablespoons flour
- ½ teaspoon salt
- ½ teaspoon pepper
- 2 pounds chicken breasts, sliced and pounded thin
- 2 tablespoons butter
- 2 tablespoons extra-virgin olive oil
- ¼ cup finely diced onion
- ¼ cup capers in brine (or a 3- to 4-ounce jar)
- ½ cup fresh-squeezed lemon juice

1. Mix flour, salt, and pepper in a shallow dish.

2. Dredge chicken breasts in flour, coating both sides evenly.

3. In a large skillet, melt butter in olive oil until both are heated.

4. Brown chicken cutlets, about 3 to 4 minutes on each side.

5. Remove chicken and keep warm.

6. Add onion to oil and butter. Cook until onion is translucent, about 5 to 6 minutes.

7. Add in capers and lemon juice. Cook 1 to 2 minutes, until sauce slightly thickens.

8. Return chicken to the pan and heat through.

Easy Vegetable Lasagna

Easy Vegetable Lasagna

This lasagna takes away all the heavy ingredients found in so many recipes and is lighter and more flavorful. It incorporates more flavor and nutrition by adding in vegetables and changing to cottage cheese instead of traditional Ricotta. Using no-boil noodles and a food processor cuts the prep time in half. Add ingredients like more vegetables (e.g., mushrooms, eggplant) or more textures. Experiment with different cheeses for more sharp flavors or use different seasonal tomatoes to change up the sauce. Try adding my pesto for a unique layer of flavor (See my post for Perfect Pesto) or try different combinations of herbs. This dish can also be made gluten-free or vegan.

Makes 8-10 servings

Vegetable Layer

- 2 tablespoons extra-virgin olive oil
- 2 large carrots, chopped (about ¾ to 1 cup)
- 1 medium zucchini, chopped
- 1 medium yellow zucchini, chopped
- 1 medium yellow onion, chopped
- ½ teaspoon salt
- ½ cup baby spinach, chopped

Sauce Layer

- 1 28-ounce can diced tomatoes (petite diced works best)
- extra-virgin olive oil
- 2 cloves garlic, minced
- ½ teaspoon salt
- ½ cup parsley, chopped
- ¼ cup basil, chopped

Cheese Layer

- 2 cups low-fat cottage cheese
- Salt & pepper to taste

Noodles

- 10-12 lasagna noodles (No Boil, partially cooked al dente, whole wheat, or gluten-free)

Topping

- 1½ cup part-skim mozzarella cheese, freshly grated or shredded (avoid the pre-packaged grated or shredded cheeses, if possible; it melts better when you grate it yourself)

1. Preheat oven to 425°.

2. Prepare the vegetables: In a medium to large skillet over medium-high heat, heat the extra-virgin olive oil. Add the carrots, zucchinis, onion, and salt and cook 8 to 10 minutes, stirring occasionally, until slightly softened.

3. Gradually add in spinach, stirring frequently until spinach is wilted. Repeat until all the spinach is used. Remove from heat and set aside.

4. Prepare the sauce: Drain off the excess liquid from the tomatoes. Add the diced and drained tomatoes to the bowl of a food processor. Add the garlic, salt, parsley, and basil. Pulse 8 to 10 times until the mixture is broken down but not watery. Pour into a bowl and set aside. Wipe out the inside of the food processor bowl.

5. Prepare the cheese: Add 1 cup cottage cheese to food processor bowl and pulse until smooth but not watery. Transfer to a large mixing bowl and

wipe out the inside of the food processor bowl.

6. Add the cooked vegetables and spinach mixture to the food processor bowl. Pulse until finely chopped (about 4 to 6 times) but not puréed or watery. Add the vegetable mix to the cottage cheese in the large mixing bowl. Add in the last 1 cup of cottage cheese, salt, and pepper, and stir to combine.

7. Assemble: Spread ½ cup of the tomato sauce on the bottom of a lasagna dish (typically 7x6 inches) or a 9x13 baking pan.

8. Layer 3 lasagna noodles on top of tomato sauce, overlapping or cutting to evenly fit to the edges.

9. Spread ½ the cheese mixture evenly over the noodles.

10. Add ¾ cup tomato sauce over the top of the cheese mixture and sprinkle with ½ cup of the grated mozzarella cheese.

11. Top with 3 more lasagna noodles, followed by the remaining cheese mixture and a ½ cup of the grated mozzarella. There's no tomato sauce in this layer on purpose!

12. Top with 3 more lasagna noodles. Spread ¾ cup tomato sauce over the top to cover the noodles. Sprinkle with 1 cup grated mozzarella cheese.

13. Cover the top with a piece of parchment paper then a large sheet of aluminum foil (do not let the foil touch the tomato sauce).

14. Bake covered 20 minutes. Uncover, rotate pan, and cook another 15 minutes, until the top is brown and bubbly.

15. Cool 15 to 20 minutes then slice and serve. Garnish with additional

parsley, basil, or cheese. Serve with a green salad or steamed green vegetables.

Grilled Salmon with Avocado Bruschetta

Grilled Salmon with Avocado Bruschetta

One of the easiest and most versatile fish to cook is salmon. It holds up well to grilling, broiling, baking, or sautéing. What makes this dish unique is the protein it packs from both the salmon and the avocado. The bruschetta on top of the warm salmon is a wonderful contrast that makes this meal perfect for a simple dinner, a main course when entertaining, or an ideal meal for dining outdoors, at the beach, or as an easy lunch.

Makes 4 servings

Bruschetta

- ¼ cup finely chopped red onion
- 1 tablespoon extra-virgin olive oil
- 1 tablespoon balsamic vinegar
- ¼ teaspoon salt
- ¼ teaspoon fresh black pepper
- 4 Roma or 2 medium tomatoes, seeded and diced
- 2 cloves garlic, minced

Salmon

- 4 wild salmon filets (about 6 to 7 ounces each)
- 2 tablespoons extra-virgin olive oil
- ¼ teaspoon kosher salt
- ¼ teaspoon fresh black pepper
- ½ teaspoon sweet paprika

Additional Ingredients

- 1 medium avocado, pit removed and diced
- 2 tablespoons chopped fresh parsley

1. Make bruschetta: In a small bowl, combine red onion, extra-virgin olive oil, balsamic vinegar, salt, and pepper. Set aside.

2. In a large bowl, add chopped tomatoes, garlic, onion mixture, and additional salt and pepper, if needed, and stir gently to combine. Cover and set aside for 10 minutes or refrigerate for 30 minutes.

Salmon

1. Preheat an outdoor grill, broiler, or a grill pan over medium heat.

2. Rub the salmon filets with extra-virgin olive oil to avoid the fish sticking to the grill or pan. Season all sides with salt, pepper, and paprika. If preferred, remove the skin.

3. Grill over low heat, under the broiler, or in a grill pan for 3 to 4 minutes per side (if keeping skin on, grill the skin side first then flip).

4. Remove from the grill, broiler, or grill pan and allow to rest for 5 minutes.

Assembly

1. Add diced avocado to the bruschetta mixture and stir to combine. (Or sprinkle the avocado on top of the bruschetta after it's spread on top of the salmon filets for an additional creamy texture and taste.)

2. Spoon a generous portion of the bruschetta on top of each salmon filet. Serve along side a green salad, roasted green beans, or three bean salad, or toasted pita triangles. Garnish with chopped parsley.

Maple Mustard Chicken

Maple Mustard Chicken

This chicken dish combines maple and mustard to create a creamy sauce that's not heavy or laden with fat and calories. The entire meal takes only minutes to prep and then cooks quickly in the oven. It's a perfect make-ahead meal and can also be doubled to serve a large family or as a main dish for a dinner party.

Makes 4 to 6 servings

- 2 pounds skinless, boneless chicken thighs (about 4 to 6)
- 1/3 cup maple syrup (natural is best, but you can use any kind of maple syrup)
- ¼ cup Dijon or grainy mustard
- ½ tablespoon apple cider vinegar
- ½ teaspoon salt
- ¼ teaspoon fresh black pepper

1. Preheat oven to 400°. Place rack in the middle of the oven.

2. Clean the chicken and pat dry. Set aside.

3. In a large bowl, whisk together maple syrup, mustard, apple cider vinegar, salt, and pepper. Add chicken to the bowl and toss to coat.

4. Spray a 9x13-inch baking dish with vegetable spray or olive oil. Transfer the chicken to the baking dish, arranging thighs in a single layer.

5. Bake 20 to 25 minutes or until meat thermometer registers 160°.

6. Serve with steamed vegetables or sautéed zucchini.

Pasta Primavera

Pasta Primavera

Squashes are high in vitamins A and C, plus high in potassium and fiber. The idea for primavera is to take different vegetables, like squashes, and sauté them together with seasoning. This primavera is an ideal meal because it can be added to pasta, brown rice, quinoa, farro, or eaten alone in a bowl with a sprinkle of fresh-grated cheese, chopped basil, or parsley.

Makes 4 to 6 servings

- 2 cups whole-wheat pasta (penne, linguine, or spaghetti)
- 1 tablespoon olive oil
- 1 medium green zucchini diced into 1-inch cubes (small and larger zucchini are more flavorful)
- 1 medium yellow zucchini, diced into 1-inch cubes
- 2 medium carrots, peeled and sliced on the diagonal into discs
- 1 medium onion, sliced
- 1 teaspoon salt
- $1/2$ teaspoon black pepper
- 1-2 cloves of garlic, finely chopped
- 1 teaspoon oregano
- 1 tablespoon chopped fresh parsley or basil (optional)
- 1 tablespoon fresh grated Parmesan cheese or Pecorino Romano cheese (optional)

1. Cook pasta according to package directions. Drain well and set aside. Reserve 1 cup of the pasta water and set aside.

2. Heat olive oil in a large skillet over medium heat. When the pan is heated, add green and yellow zucchini, carrots, onion and oregano.

3. Sprinkle with salt and pepper.

4. Cover. Cook over medium heat for 10 to 15 minutes, stirring occasionally. (Cook for less time if you prefer your vegetables crispy or al dente; cook longer if you like your vegetables softer.)

5. When vegetables are cooked to desired consistency, add in the chopped garlic.Cook an additional 1 to 2 minutes, until garlic is fragrant.

6. Add in the cooked pasta. Toss together.

7. Serve in bowls or on plates. Sprinkle pasta with grated cheese and chopped parsley or basil if using.

Peanut Chicken Lettuce Wraps

Peanut Chicken Lettuce Wraps

This dish is perfect to satisfy a craving for something that's sweet, tangy, and delicious at the same time. This recipe is simple and quick to make, plus it's low-carb and full of protein.

Makes 4 to 6 servings

Sauce

- 3 tablespoons creamy peanut butter (any brand)
- 1 tablespoon low-sodium soy sauce
- 1 tablespoon fresh-squeezed lime juice
- 1 tablespoon brown sugar
- 1 to 2 teaspoons sriracha (optional)
- 1 teaspoon fresh grated ginger

Chicken

- 1 tablespoon light olive oil
- 1 tablespoon sesame oil
- 1 pound lean ground chicken
- 1 carrot, peeled and diced
- 1 shallot, diced
- 2 garlic cloves, minced
- 1 tablespoon fresh-grated ginger
- ¼ cup hoisin sauce
- 1 teaspoon fish sauce (optional)
- 1 to 2 teaspoons sriracha (optional)
- 2 tablespoons chopped fresh cilantro
- 1 head Bibb lettuce

1. Prepare the sauce: Whisk peanut butter, soy sauce, lime juice, brown sugar, and sriracha, if using. Add tablespoons of water until desired thickness. Set aside.

2. In a large skillet over medium-high heat (or in a wok), heat the olive oil and sesame oil. Add the chicken, carrot, and shallot. Cook until the chicken is browned and no longer pink, about 5 to 8 minutes.

3. Add garlic and ginger and cook 1 minute.

4. Stir in hoisin sauce, fish sauce, and sriracha, if using, and cook until heated through, about 1 to 2 minutes. Remove from heat and stir in cilantro.

5. Serve rounded spoonfuls of the chicken mixture inside the center of each lettuce leaf. Drizzle with the peanut sauce or roll the lettuce leaf like a taco, a slice of pizza, or a burrito, and dip into the peanut sauce.

Perfect Pesto

Perfect Pesto

Pesto is a wonderful sauce that compliments so many types of food. This sauce is the right balance of ingredients to keep the pesto tasting fresh and herbal but without the strong bite or after taste of the garlic. Try this sauce over your favorite pasta or use it as a spread for sandwiches instead of mayonnaise. Try it tossed with shrimp or spread lightly over roasted chicken. It goes great with roasted potatoes or roasted vegetables, like broccoli. For extra sweetness, try tossing in ½ cup of thawed, cooked, or leftover peas. In the spring or summer, add in fresh mint leaves from the garden to create a smoother, sweeter taste.

Makes 4 to 6 servings

- 2 cups fresh basil (leaves only, stems removed)
- ½ cup fresh spinach (leaves only, stems removed)
- ½ cup thawed green peas
- ¼ cup fresh mint leaves
- 2 tablespoons toasted pine nuts or walnuts
- 2 medium garlic cloves, peeled
- ½ cup extra-virgin olive oil
- ½ cup fresh-grated Parmesan (avoid using commercially-packaged grated Parmesan. Fresh works best!)

1. Combine basil, spinach, peas, mint, nuts and garlic in a food processor. Process until finely minced.

2. While the processor is running on low, slowly drizzle in the extra-virgin olive oil through the feed tube until the mixture is smooth.

3. Add the cheese and process on low for 30 to 45 seconds to combine.

4. Store in the refrigerator up to 1 week or in the freezer for up to 2 weeks.

Serving suggestions: Toss with your favorite pasta or use as a topping for grilled or baked chicken, pork, salmon, or shrimp. It works great as a spread for sandwiches or a healthier alternative to mayonnaise.

Pork Pot Roast

Pork Pot Roast

Traditional pot roast uses different cuts of beef to slowly cook in a rich sauce with vegetables and different seasonings. This recipe uses pork instead of beef. Choose any cut of pork you prefer, like shoulder, picnic cut, loin, or roast. Instead of carrots, celery, and potatoes, this recipe uses flavorful root vegetables like rutabaga, onions, and parsnips that meld together to make a delicious sauce and side dish. Add in unique seasonings, like garlic, bay leaf, and some apple cider vinegar to bring out the flavor of the braising sauce and vegetables. This recipe can be customized in so many ways—add tomatoes, different types of potatoes, jicama, apples, pears, peas, or any kind of greens.

Makes 4 to 6 servings

- 3- to 4-pound pork roast (or shoulder)
- Salt & pepper
- 2 tablespoons olive oil
- 4 large carrots, cut into 1-inch pieces
- 2 large parsnips, cut into 1-inch pieces
- 1 large onion, cut into 8 pieces
- 3 rutabagas or yellow turnips, cut into 1-inch pieces
- 2 garlic cloves, coarsely chopped
- 2 bay leaves
- ¼ cup apple cider vinegar
- 2 cups low-sodium chicken broth
- Optional: ¼ cup dry white wine

1. Preheat oven to 300°.

2. Salt and pepper all sides of the roast. Heat olive oil over medium-high heat in a large Dutch oven.

3. Brown the roast on all four sides, 3 to 4 minutes per side. Set aside on a platter.

4. Add all of the vegetables, garlic and bay leaves to the Dutch oven and stir to combine. Add apple cider vinegar and combine.

5. Add chicken broth (and wine, if using) and stir to combine. Nestle pork roast on top of vegetables, cover, and cook for 2 hours.

6. Remove from oven and let stand for 20 minutes.

7. Place meat on a platter and surround with the vegetables. Drizzle the meat and vegetables with sauce or juices. Slice and serve.

Quick & Easy Shrimp

Quick & Easy Shrimp

Fresh shrimp gives this recipe a wonderful, caramelized sauce that pairs wonderfully with any type of crispy green vegetable, like green beans, broccoli, or even Brussels sprouts.

Makes 4 to 6 servings

- 2 tablespoons of minced garlic
- 1 teaspoon ground ginger
- ½ cup honey
- ¼ cup low-sodium soy sauce
- 1 pound medium shrimp, uncooked, shelled, and deveined
- 1½ cup green beans, broccoli, or Brussels sprouts

1. Prepare the sauce: In a small bowl, combine garlic, ginger, honey, and soy sauce. Set aside.

2. Place the shrimp in a medium bowl. Pour ⅓ of the sauce on the shrimp and toss to coat. Cover with plastic wrap and refrigerate for up to 1 hour.

3. After the shrimp has been marinated, heat a nonstick medium (about 10 inches) skillet over medium-high heat. Add 2 tablespoons of the sauce into the skillet and heat until steaming or slightly sizzling.

4. Toss in the green vegetable of choice and cook until tender, about 6 to 8 minutes, depending on the vegetable used. Remove and set aside.

5. Take shrimp out of the marinade sauce and, in 2 batches (5 to 10 shrimp per batch), cook 1 to 2 minutes per side until the shrimp are browned and begin to curl. Do not overcook! Take the shrimp out of the pan and place onto a plate and set aside.

6. When the shrimp are all cooked, return the vegetables to the skillet and heat through. Add the shrimp back into the skillet. Add any remaining sauce. Heat for 2 to 3 minutes, tossing to coat the shrimp and the vegetables in the caramelized sauce.

7. Serve over brown rice or soba noodles. Drizzle any remaining sauce from the skillet over the shrimp and vegetables.

Skillet Chicken & Brussels Sprouts

Skillet Chicken & Brussels Sprouts

Skillet chicken and Brussels sprouts provide enough protein, fiber, iron, and other key nutrients without added fat, salt, or sugars, and it's easy to make. The recipe can be doubled or tripled, and any leftovers can be frozen for up to two months in an airtight container.

Makes 2 to 4 servings

- 2 to 4 large chicken thighs, bone in and skin on
- Salt & pepper to taste
- Nonstick cooking spray or 1 teaspoon of olive oil
- 2 slices of turkey bacon (optional)
- 1½ to 2 cups Brussels sprouts, trimmed and quartered
- 1 medium apple, cored and cut into 8 to 10 slices
- 1 tablespoon red wine vinegar
- ¼ cup apple juice

1. Preheat oven to 425°.

2. Pat chicken thighs dry with paper towels then season both sides with salt and pepper.

3. Heat a large oven-proof skillet (preferably nonstick or cast iron) over medium-high heat. Add chicken thighs, skin side down, to the skillet and cook for about 3 minutes or until edges start to brown.

4. Without turning chicken, add in the bacon, if using, and cook 2 more minutes. Remove from heat. Add Brussels sprouts and apple slices.

5. Stir Brussels sprouts and apple slices around. Season lightly with salt and pepper.

6. Place the skillet in the preheated oven and cook for about 10 minutes.

7. Remove the skillet from the oven. Be careful! The pan will be extremely hot! Stir the Brussels sprouts and apples. Turn the chicken over. Return skillet to the oven for an additional 10 minutes.

8. Remove from the oven. Again, the pan will be hot! Let it rest about 5 minutes. Move the chicken to a plate. Using a slotted spoon, remove the Brussels sprouts and apples to a second plate. Leave as much of the juice in the pan as you can.

9. Carefully put the skillet back on the stove on low heat. Carefully add in the red wine vinegar to deglaze the bottom of the pan. Scrape the bottom to loosen any bits of chicken or vegetables.

10. Once the pan is deglazed (about 10 to 30 seconds), pour in the apple juice. Reduce to a simmer and cook about 2 to 5 minutes, until sauce thickens and takes on a syrup-like consistency. Spoon over the chicken, Brussels sprouts, and apple pieces.

Skillet Chicken with Tomato & Spinach

Skillet Chicken with Tomato & Spinach

The chicken in this dish is lean and provides protein and energy, while the tomatoes and spinach provide fiber, vitamins, and minerals. Even better, this dish is ready in under 30 minutes, and it's made in one skillet so cleanup is easy. Or, make a tray of this to have on hand for meals throughout the week.

Makes 4 servings

- 1 tablespoon extra-virgin olive oil
- 4 boneless, skinless chicken breasts pounded thin
- 1 clove garlic, finely minced
- ½ teaspoon dried oregano
- ½ teaspoon salt
- ¼ teaspoon pepper
- ¼ cup low-sodium chicken broth or water
- 2 medium plum tomatoes, sliced
- 1 bag (about 6 ounces) of fresh baby spinach leaves

1. In a large nonstick skillet, heat oil over medium heat.

2. Sprinkle chicken breasts with garlic, oregano, salt, and pepper. Add chicken breasts to skillet and cook over medium heat 6 to 8 minutes on each side, until juices are clear.

3. Stir broth or water into skillet slowly.

4. Top chicken breasts with tomato slices; cover and cook over medium-high heat for 2 to 3 minutes, until tomatoes are heated through.

5. Add spinach around chicken; cover and cook 2 to 3 additional minutes, until spinach is wilted.

6. Serve warm with a small side salad or additional steamed vegetables.

Slow Cooker Beef Burgundy

Slow Cooker Beef Burgundy

Beef Burgundy is a classic French recipe. Cuts of beef and vegetables are slowly braised in a rich sauce that is typically made with wine. The ingredients in this dish are simple. The vegetables provide fiber, vitamins, and minerals, while the meat adds protein. You can use any vegetables you choose or try experimenting with different combinations of celery, carrots, onion, parsnips, or potatoes. Don't be afraid to use wine. The alcohol content gets cooked off,and it adds delicate layers of flavor to the sauce. The secret ingredient in this recipe is golden raisins—they add a unique layer of flavor and help brighten the sauce. Serve this meal in a bowl over rice or quinoa, toast points, toasted pita triangles, or even pasta. Garnish with parsley or any fresh chopped herbs.

Makes 6 servings

- 2 pounds beef chuck cut into 1-inch chunks
- 3 tablespoons all-purpose flour, divided
- 1 teaspoon paprika
- 2 tablespoons extra-virgin olive oil, divided
- 1 large onion, diced
- 1 cup sliced fresh mushrooms
- 1½ teaspoons dried thyme
- 1½ cups red wine (Cabernet, Merlot, or Burgundy)
- 3 carrots, chopped
- 2 celery stalks, chopped
- 1 6-ounce can tomato paste
- ½ cup golden raisins
- 1½ teaspoons salt
- 1 teaspoon black pepper
- 2 tablespoons unsalted butter, softened
- ¼ cup chopped fresh parsley and extra for garnish

1. Put chunks of beef into a resealable plastic bag. Add 1 tablespoon flour and the paprika. Seal the bag and toss the beef to coat all surfaces with the flour and paprika mixture. Remove the beef from the bag, shake off any excess flour, and set aside.

2. Heat 1 tablespoon extra-virgin olive oil in a large skillet over medium-high heat. Add the beef to the skillet, stirring occasionally, until the beef is seared and browned on all sides and no longer pink on the outside, about 6 to 8 minutes. Transfer the beef to the cooking insert of a slow cooker.

3. Lower the heat under the skillet to medium. Heat the remaining 1 tablespoon of extra-virgin olive oil and add onion, mushrooms, and thyme. Cook, stirring often, until the vegetables begin to soften, about 5 minutes. Add to the beef in the slow cooker.

4. Add the wine, carrots, celery, tomato paste, raisins, salt, and pepper to the beef and vegetables in the slow cooker. Stir all ingredients to combine.

5. Cover and set the timer for 6 hours on the slow cooker's lowest setting.

6. After 5 hours, mash the remaining 2 tablespoons of flour and the softened butter together in a small dish or bowl until smooth. Stir the flour and butter mixture into the cooking stew in the slow cooker until it dissolves. Cover and allow the beef burgundy to finish cooking.

7. When finished, stir in the chopped fresh parsley and serve. Garnish with additional parsley or any other chopped fresh herbs.

Soba Noodles & Vegetables

Soba Noodles & Vegetables

Soba noodles, unlike commercial pasta products, are made from buckwheat. While not a true low-calorie or low-carbohydrate food, soba noodles have half the unhealthy carbohydrates and calories as commercial pasta. Soba noodles are high in necessary fiber and magnesium, gluten-free, easy to cook, and contain a nutty, earthy flavor that makes them a delicious alternative to plain pasta.

Makes 2 to 4 servings

Vegetables

- 2½ cups sugar snap peas
- 2 cups of frozen edamame, thawed
- 4 carrots, peeled

Sauce

- ¼ cup low-sodium soy sauce
- 2 tablespoons extra-virgin olive oil
- 1 small lime, juiced
- 1 tablespoon sesame oil
- 1 tablespoon honey
- 2½ teaspoons fresh-grated ginger

Noodles

- ¼ cup sesame seeds (can be white, black, or mixed)
- 6-8 ounces of soba noodles
- ½ cup chopped parsley

1. Prepare the vegetables in advance. Slice the sugar snap peas in half lengthwise or in a rough chop and slice the carrots into thin strips or use the vegetable peeler to make carrot ribbons.

2. Prepare the sauce: Whisk together all sauce ingredients in a small bowl; set aside.

3. Bring two pots of water to a boil (one large and one medium).

4. Toast the sesame seeds in a small pan over medium heat, approximately 4 to 5 minutes. Move or stir the seeds frequently to prevent burning. Hint: when the white seeds turn golden or light brown, they're done.

5. Cook the soba noodles in the large pot per the package instructions. Drain and rinse with cool water.

6. Cook the edamame in the medium pot for about 4 to 5 minutes. Add in the halved or chopped sugar snap peas and cook for 30 seconds to 1 minute. Once the sugar snap peas look vibrantly green, drain.

7. Combine the soba noodles, edamame, sugar snap peas, and carrots in a large bowl. Pour the sauce over and toss to combine. Add in the toasted sesame seeds and parsley and toss lightly to combine.

8. Serve in bowls and garnish with lime wedges, chopped peanuts, or alfalfa sprouts.

Sweet & Tangy Chicken

Sweet & Tangy Chicken

Many pregnant women have an unusual craving for all things sour when they're pregnant. Dinner is the perfect place to bring in sour flavors with a slight hint of sweet to complement a meal and add to the overall flavor profile. Further, recipes like these make enough servings for leftovers that can be reheated or made into small snack portions.

Makes 6 to 8 servings

- 6–8 chicken thighs, skin left on
- 1/3 cup yellow mustard
- 1/4 cup low-sodium soy sauce
- 1/4 cup light brown sugar, firmly packed
- 1/4 cup white vinegar
- 2 tablespoons honey
- 1/2 teaspoon garlic powder
- 1/4 teaspoon salt
- Pinch of black pepper

1. Preheat oven to 400°.

2. Clean and dry the chicken breasts.

3. In a medium bowl, combine the mustard, soy sauce, brown sugar, white vinegar, honey, garlic powder, salt, and pepper.

4. Add chicken to the mustard mixture and toss to coat.

5. Arrange chicken on a baking sheet and bake skin side up for 40 minutes. Turn chicken halfway through.

6. Turn up oven temperature to 500°. Turn the chicken back to skin side up

and cook 5 to 10 minutes, until skin begins to crisp.

7. Serve over brown rice, quinoa, farro, a salad, or spinach.

The Best Turkey Burger

The Best Turkey Burger

The seasonings in this burger are a wonderful combination of flavors that taste delicious but are subtle enough to not overpower the meal. With the combination of brining and seasonings, you have the best turkey burger... ever! Add your own combinations of seasonings or experiment with the amounts to create different flavor profiles. This burger pairs well with multiple condiments or side dishes, including green salads, simple pasta salads, roasted vegetables, or fruits. Try it as a main meal or a simple lunch. Eat it alone or pair it with a multigrain roll, a pita bread, or freshly made croutons.

Makes 4 turkey burgers

- 1 pound ground turkey
- 1 teaspoon baking soda
- ¼ cup water
- 2 teaspoons Dijon mustard
- 1 teaspoon freshly ground black pepper
- ½ teaspoon onion powder
- ½ teaspoon salt
- ½ teaspoon sweet paprika
- ½ teaspoon garlic powder
- Vegetable spray
- Optional: 1 egg for binding

1. To brine, place the turkey in a bowl. Sprinkle with baking soda. Pour water over turkey, mix lightly to coat. Do not submerge the meat in water. The water and baking soda mixture should just coat the meat. Cover lightly with plastic wrap or foil. Set aside for 30 minutes to one hour.

2. After the turkey has brined, drain any excess water and transfer turkey to a large bowl.

3. Add all remaining ingredients and stir gently to combine. To avoid a dense burger, don't squeeze the mix tightly while combining and avoid overmixing. An additional egg, if using, may be needed to keep the mix combined.

4. Split the mix into 4 equal portions. Pat each portion into a burger patty. Place patties in the refrigerator to set, 30 to 45 minutes.

5. Preheat the grill, skillet, or grill pan over medium-high heat. Spray with vegetable spray.

6. Cook each patty 4 to 6 minutes per side, until no longer pink or the temperature reads 160°.

7. Assemble on a toasted multigrain roll or over a tossed green salad.

Suggested toppings: pesto (see my recipe for Perfect Pesto!), diced tomatoes, fresh guacamole, cheese (Monterey Jack, Fontina, or white cheddar), ketchup, Greek yogurt, hummus, or lettuce (Bibb, Romaine, or a mesclun mix).

Tilapia with Tomato & Broccoli

Tilapia with Tomatoes & Broccoli

Tilapia is a safe fish for pregnant women to consume, and it contains key nutrients like Omega-3 fatty acids, protein, and other vitamins. What makes this recipe unique is that instead of using lots of pots and pans, all you need is a baking sheet and a large piece of parchment paper. All the ingredients go into the parchment paper that gets tightly folded to perfectly steam the fish and the vegetables. A few other ingredients add lots of great flavor.

Makes 2 to 4 servings

- 2 tilapia filets
- Salt & pepper
- 20 cherry tomatoes, halved
- 2 cups of broccoli florets and diced stems
- 4 cloves of garlic, sliced thinly
- ¼ cup chopped fresh parsley
- 2 tablespoons extra-virgin olive oil
- 2 teaspoons low-sodium soy sauce
- 2 tablespoons rice vinegar
- 2 cups cooked brown rice (optional)

1. Preheat oven to 400°. Place a 12-inch square of parchment paper on a baking sheet.

2. Season the tilapia on both sides with salt and pepper.

3. Place both pieces of tilapia on one side of the parchment sheet. Cover with the tomatoes, broccoli, garlic, and parsley.

4. Pour the extra-virgin olive oil, soy sauce, and rice vinegar over the fish and vegetables.

5. Fold the other half of the parchment paper over the fish and vegetables and fold and tuck the edges tightly to seal the parchment packet.

6. Bake for 10 minutes. Allow to cool for 2 minutes.

7. Carefully pierce the top of the parchment pack and slowly tear open. Serve the fish, vegetables, and sauce over brown rice, if desired, or together in a bowl or shallow plate.

Tofu Stir Fry

Tofu Stir Fry

Eaten plain, tofu is essentially tasteless and has a smooth, nondescript texture. However, when you cook with tofu, it is a lot like pasta or rice. It absorbs the flavors of whatever you're cooking and magnifies the taste. Tofu is a terrific substitute for animal protein sources. This recipe combines mild flavors that work well together. Prefer spicy or more flavor? This recipe works well with an additional sprinkle of crushed red pepper, a drizzle of sriracha, or an extra squeeze of lime juice. It pairs very well with brown rice, quinoa, or rice noodles. Try adding in different flavors with optional toppings, like chopped peanuts, almonds, cashews, basil, parsley, or tarragon.

Makes 4 to 6 servings

- ¼ cup low-sodium soy sauce
- ¼ cup fresh-squeezed lime juice
- 1 tablespoon natural honey
- 2 teaspoons fresh-grated ginger
- 1 block extra-firm tofu
- 2 tablespoons sesame oil
- 2 cloves garlic, minced
- 1 small yellow onion, chopped
- 1 cup frozen shelled edamame, thawed
- 1 carrot, chopped
- 2 cups soba noodles, cooked
- 1 tablespoon sesame seeds, toasted
- Garnish (optional): chopped green onion, cilantro, basil, peanuts, cashews

1. In a medium bowl, add soy sauce, lime juice, honey, and ginger. Stir to combine and set aside.

2. Drain the tofu block and wrap in 2 paper towels or a dish towel. Place a plate (or a large can of vegetables or a small hardcover book) on top to weigh down the tofu and further drain the tofu for about 15 to 20 minutes.

3. Unwrap tofu and dice into ¼- to ½-inch cubes.

4. In a large nonstick skillet, frying pan, or wok, heat 2 tablespoons of sesame oil gently over medium heat. Be careful not to burn the oil.

5. Add tofu and fry in the oil, stirring occasionally, about 5 minutes, until browned.

6. Add garlic and onion. Cook 1 to 2 minutes, stirring occasionally, until softened.

7. Add in edamame and carrot and cook until tender, about 2 to 4 minutes.

8. Add soba noodles, soy sauce mixture, and sesame seeds. Cook 1 to 2 minutes, stirring occasionally.

9. Remove from heat.

10. Garnish with green onions, cilantro, basil, or nuts.

Tri-Color Frittata

Tri-Color Frittata

This frittata is colorful and boasts flavors that go amazingly well to-gether—egg, tomato, and spinach. Basil gives it a wonderful aroma and smooth taste to round out the earthiness of the spinach. Try experimenting with different vegetables, herbs, or finely cut or diced pieces of meat. Try this dish for a weekend brunch or weeknight meal or bring it with you if you're invited to a brunch or party. It also makes an easy dish to bring someone who has no time to cook or is feeling under the weather or just needs a break from cooking.

Makes 6 to 8 servings

- 1 tablespoon extra-virgin olive oil
- ½ cup chopped onion
- 1 cup spinach, chopped
- 8 egg whites, slightly beaten (save the yolks—if your frittata is too pale or you like more color or protein, add in 4 yolks)
- 2 teaspoons of baking powder
- 10 cherry tomatoes, halved (or 2 Roma tomatoes sliced into circles)
- 2 ounces fresh mozzarella cheese, shredded
- Basil or parsley for garnish

1. Heat oven to 425°.

2. In a medium skillet, heat extra-virgin olive oil over medium heat.

3. Add onions and cook 5 to 7 minutes, until softened.

4. Add spinach and cook until wilted, about 2 minutes.

5. Mix baking powder into egg whites or egg mixture. Pour egg whites (or egg mixture if using yolks) over onion and spinach mix. Scatter tomatoes

and mozzarella cheese over the top.

6. Lower heat and cook about 5 minutes, until the edges of the egg and vegetable mix begin to set or the outer ½- to 1-inch of the mixture looks firm and set.

7. Transfer skillet to the oven. Cook 5 to 10 minutes, until mixture is firmly set.

8. Remove from oven and cool slightly.

9. Slide frittata out of the pan onto cutting board or serving platter or slice it carefully from the skillet.

10. Cut into slices and serve with multigrain toast or toasted semolina bread slices. Or serve with a fresh green or kale salad. Garnish with basil or parsley.

Vegetable Casserole

Vegetable Casserole

This casserole is packed with healthy nutrients and fiber. The vegetables, when layered and cooked slowly in the oven, blend together to create incredible flavors and work great as a main course or side dish. It's perfect reheated or as a lunch, as a brunch dish, as an entrée at a party, or to bring to someone who is vegetarian or gluten-free. You can use any kind of vegetables that are in season, and it works very well with fall root vegetables, spring greens, or even adding in some of summer's best fruits or vegetables.

Makes 6 servings

- 7 tablespoons extra-virgin olive oil, separated, plus 1 teaspoon
- 2 medium green zucchinis, sliced into ¼-inch strips lengthwise
- 2 medium narrow eggplants, seeded and sliced into ¼-inch thick strips lengthwise
- Salt & pepper to taste
- 1 medium shallot, minced
- 2 garlic cloves, sliced
- 1 pound (about 10 to 12) plum (Roma) tomatoes, seeded and diced into ½-inch cubes
- 6 ounces fontina cheese, shredded
- ¼ cup chopped fresh basil
- ⅓ cup Panko or dried seasoned breadcrumbs

1. Preheat oven to 425°.

2. Grease 2 baking sheets with one tablespoon of extra-virgin olive oil on each. Put zucchini slices on one sheet and eggplant slices on the second sheet. Brush the slices with 1 tablespoon extra-virgin olive oil and season with salt and pepper. Bake 15 minutes, until vegetable slices are tender. Remove from oven and allow to cool slightly.

3. In a large skillet, heat 2 tablespoons of extra-virgin olive oil over medium-high heat. Add the shallots and cook until softened, about 3 to 4 minutes. Add tomatoes and cook until slightly softened, about 2 to 3 minutes. Season with additional salt and pepper.

4. Grease a baking dish (8x8-inch for a thicker casserole or 9x13-inch for a thinner, shorter casserole) with vegetable spray or an additional teaspoon of extra-virgin olive oil. Layer half the eggplant and spread ¼ of the tomato mixture on top. Scatter half the fontina cheese and basil next.

5. Layer half the zucchini and then an additional ¼ cup of the tomato mixture, remaining basil, eggplant, and zucchini. Top with any remaining tomato mixture and fontina cheese.

6. Mix panko breadcrumbs and 1 tablespoon of extra-virgin olive oil and sprinkle over casserole.

7. Bake for 20 to 25 minutes, until bubbly and crisp. Remove from oven and let stand 5 to 10 minutes before slicing and serving. Serve hot or warm.

Serve with a fresh green salad, tossed mesclun salad, alongside fresh fruit, or with a piece of toasted whole-grain bread.

V

Vegetables & Salads

Avocado Salad with Couscous

Avocado Salad with Couscous

Avocados are a great source of healthy fat. They're packed with protein and fiber, plus other essential nutrients. They pair well with tomatoes or other vegetables, herbs, nuts, or grains. This salad provides fiber and additional healthy carbohydrates to make this salad satisfying and delicious. The black beans provide additional protein, fiber, and flavor.

Makes 4 to 6 servings

- 1 cup Israeli couscous
- 1 tomato, chopped
- 1 cup canned black beans, rinsed and drained
- 1 cup whole kernel corn
- 2 scallions, chopped
- 1 tablespoon cilantro or parsley, chopped
- 1 medium lime, juiced
- ½ cup salsa (fresh or store bought)
- Salt & pepper to taste
- 1 avocado, seeded and chopped

1. Cook couscous according to package directions. Set aside to cool.

2. In a large bowl, combine tomato, black beans, corn, scallions, cilantro or parsley, lime juice, and salsa.

3. Add couscous and toss to combine. Season with salt and pepper to taste. Add extra lime juice if needed.

4. Add chopped avocado and serve immediately.

Citrus Zucchini Salad

Citrus Zucchini Salad

Using zucchini in place of pasta provides more nutrients and fiber than traditional pasta, is gluten-free, fat free, cholesterol free, and cooks quickly. Making the zucchini noodles takes a little bit of work. There are several useful, safe gadgets available that let you simply insert the zucchini in one end and, by either twisting or cranking a handle, yields perfect tendrils of zucchini noodles on the other end. Or, if you can't find one of those gadgets or don't want to be bothered making your own, there are now several options for zucchini noodles available from popular food manufacturers in the frozen food department. Fresh is best, but, in this case, the frozen version is just as good.

Makes 4-6 servings

- 3 tablespoons extra-virgin olive oil, divided (2 tablespoons and 1 tablespoon)
- 1 clove garlic, minced
- 12 grape tomatoes, halved
- 2 medium zucchinis made into noodles (or use frozen, cooked according to package directions)
- Salt and pepper
- ½ cup pine nuts, lightly toasted (optional)
- 2 tablespoons each fresh orange and lemon juice
- ½ teaspoon each of orange and lemon zest
- ½ cup grated Parmesan cheese

1. In a medium skillet, heat 2 tablespoons extra-virgin olive oil over medium heat.

2. Add garlic and tomato halves. Sauté for 2 minutes to avoid burning the garlic.

3. Add zucchini noodles and season with salt and pepper.

4. Add 1 tablespoon extra-virgin olive oil and cook for 5 minutes or until the noodles are firm but translucent.

5.Add orange juice and lemon juice and the orange and lemon zests. Toss with the pine nuts (if desired).

Easiest Baked Eggplant

Easiest Baked Eggplant

This is one of the easiest eggplant dishes. The eggplant is delicious, crispy, and not greasy. While not the traditional way to make baked eggplant, this dish loses all the bad fats used for frying and cuts down on the prep time. The simple marinara sauce is rich, easy to prepare, and gives you some leftover sauce to use later or freeze. This meal is perfect for reheating and it can be made in advance and frozen. It can be doubled for feeding larger crowds and is perfect to bring to a party or as a complete dinner for a family.

Makes 6 servings

- 2 medium eggplants, peeled and sliced into ½-inch rounds
- 4 tablespoons low-fat mayonnaise
- ½ cup seasoned breadcrumbs

Sauce

- 2 tablespoons extra-virgin olive oil
- 2 cloves garlic, minced
- 1 28-ounce can crushed tomatoes
- 1 28-ounce can tomato purée
- 2 tablespoons dried oregano
- 2 tablespoons dried parsley or ¼ cup chopped fresh parsley
- 2 bay leaves
- 1 teaspoon onion powder
- Salt & pepper to taste

Topping

- ½ cup fresh-grated mozzarella cheese

1. Heat oven to 350°. Line 2 baking sheets with tin foil.

2. Spread a thin layer of mayonnaise on each slice of eggplant then dredge through the breadcrumbs, pressing occasionally to make the breadcrumbs adhere to the eggplant rounds.

3. Arrange the coated eggplant rounds in a single layer on the baking sheet. Bake 20 minutes, until the top layer is golden brown. Flip the rounds and cook on the other side for 20 to 25 minutes, until that side is golden brown also. Remove from heat and set aside.

4. Prepare the sauce: Heat the extra-virgin olive oil in a large saucepan over medium heat. Sauté the garlic until tender, about 3 to 4 minutes, without burning. Stir in the crushed tomatoes, tomato purée, oregano, and dried parsley (if using fresh parsley, add it last when the sauce is finished), bay leaves, and onion powder. Reduce the heat to low and simmer, covered, for 40 to 45 minutes. Add salt and pepper to taste.

5. Add 1 or 2 ladlesful of the marinara sauce to the bottom of a 9x13 baking dish or a lasagna pan. Add a layer of eggplant rounds then top with sauce. Repeat until all eggplant rounds are used or the baking dish is full. Eggplant rounds can overlap or can be cut to fit the corners of the dish or fill in gaps. Sprinkle with mozzarella cheese and cover with aluminum foil.

6. Bake for 40 minutes. Remove from oven and remove the foil. Return to the oven and cook for an additional 15 to 20 minutes, until the top is browned and bubbly. Remove from oven and allow to cool slightly for 10 to 15 minutes. Slice and serve.

Options:

For more cheese flavor, sprinkle fresh-grated Parmesan cheese on top of each eggplant round or add it to the breadcrumb mixture.

For more vegetables, add chopped spinach, Swiss chard, or peas to each eggplant layer before adding a layer of sauce.

If sauce is too chunky, use a handheld blender to carefully pulse the sauce several times to desired consistency. Or carefully spoon 2 to 3 ladlesful of sauce into a blender and pulse 2 to 4 times to desired thickness or consistency. Return the sauce to the saucepan and repeat with additional ladlesful of sauce as needed.

Tip: A simple trick for cutting eggplant into perfect slices every time is to use a ruler and measure out ½- or ¼-inch increments along the eggplant. Put a toothpick or an imprint from a fork at each measured increment. When finished, use a knife to cut at each toothpick or on each fork mark. It couldn't be easier!

Green Bean Bundles

Green Bean Bundles

Green beans are a wonderful green vegetable. Green beans are high in fiber, vitamins A and C, potassium, calcium, and iron and are fat-free. They're naturally sweet and crispy and can work in salads, as a side dish, or as a snack. The secret to this recipe is to blanch the green beans first by immersing them in boiling water for a few minutes then quickly, using an ice water bath to stop the cooking process, lock in the deep green color of the green beans and seal in the flavor. The zucchini works best when it's also pre-cooked until it's slightly browned, so it wraps easier around the bundle of green beans.

Makes 6 to 8 bundles

- 1 green zucchini, sliced into thin strips lengthwise
- ¼ cup extra-virgin olive oil
- 1½ pounds fresh green beans or haricot verts
- 1 teaspoon garlic powder
- Salt & pepper to taste
- ¼ cup chopped fresh parsley

1. Preheat oven to 400°. Place zucchini slices on a baking sheet and brush lightly with extra-virgin olive oil. Bake 6 to 8 minutes, until the zucchini is soft, pliable, and slightly browned.

2. Trim the ends off the green beans. Bring a 5-quart pot of lightly salted water to a boil.

3. Cook the green beans about 2 to 3 minutes, until slightly tender. Drain the green beans and quickly submerge into a large bowl of ice and water.

4. When the green beans are cool, drain and pat them dry. Sprinkle the garlic powder over the green beans and toss to combine.

5. Wrap a cooled piece of zucchini around the center of 6 to 8 green beans. Secure with a toothpick. Place the wrapped bundles on the baking sheet and brush with the remaining extra-virgin olive oil and sprinkle with salt and pepper. Bake 10 to 12 minutes, until the zucchini is cooked and browned.

6. Allow the bundles to cool slightly. Sprinkle with parsley before serving.

Grilled Asparagus with Quinoa Salad

Grilled Asparagus & Quinoa Salad

Quinoa has been around for centuries. It has less calories and carbohydrates than white rice but close to 5 grams of fiber and protein that rice does not. Quinoa is one of the few foods that contains all nine essential amino acids. A serving of quinoa provides protein, iron, fiber, thiamine, vitamin B6, magnesium, phosphorous, and folate. Quinoa is also gluten-free.

Quinoa alone is not that tasty. It has a nutty, earthy taste and texture that begs to be combined with other ingredients. This grilled asparagus and quinoa salad is easy to make and can be used as a side dish to bring to a picnic or family event or to have as a main course or lunch. Plus, the asparagus provides additional vitamins and fiber. The vinaigrette is made with fresh basil that can be used on salads, fish, or chicken.

Makes 4-6 servings

- 1 cup red quinoa
- 2 lemons
- 2 pounds asparagus spears (or 2 bundles)
- 5 tablespoons extra-virgin olive oil (divided)
- ½ teaspoon grated lemon zest
- Salt and pepper
- 1 plum or Roma tomato, seeded and diced
- 1 container (8 ounces) fresh mozzarella pearls (or bocconcini)

Vinaigrette

- 2 cups packed basil leaves
- 1 small clove garlic
- 3 tablespoons lemon juice
- Salt and pepper

1. Cook the quinoa according to the package directions and set aside.

2. Grate 1 teaspoon of lemon zest and set aside. Squeeze 3 tablespoons lemon juice and set aside.

3. Set grill to high (or use a grill pan over high heat on the stove).

4. Trim an inch off the bottom of the asparagus spears. Toss the spears with 2 tablespoons extra-virgin olive oil, the lemon zest, salt, and pepper.

5. Grill the asparagus spears for 3 to 4 minutes on each side, turning often to avoid burning. The asparagus should be fork-tender and have a slight char all around. Allow to cool then cut into pieces.

6. Use a food processor to make the vinaigrette: Pulse the basil, garlic, lemon juice, salt. And pepper until chopped. Slowly add in the remaining 3 tablespoons of extra-virgin olive oil until well mixed. If the mixture looks too dry, add more extra-virgin olive oil.

7. Put the cooked quinoa in a bowl. Add in the asparagus, tomato, and then the vinaigrette and toss to combine. Add the mozzarella pearls or bocconcini prior to serving.

Modern Skillet Shakshuka

Modern Skillet Shakshuka

Shakshuka is a common dish in many Middle Eastern and Mediterranean cultures. The base of shakshuka is tomatoes, and they develop into a creamy base to hold the flavors of whatever spices or seasonings you add. You can add sweet or savory spices to change the profile of the dish. There are so many ways to make this dish, and each region has its own special twist on how they do it. This recipe has plenty of dark green vegetables for texture, taste, and nutrients, like vitamins A and C, potassium, protein, iron, vitamin B6, and magnesium, and the tomato base provides vitamin C and keeps the whole mixture less bitter. It's fat free and gluten-free and can be made vegan if the eggs are removed.

Makes 4 to 6 servings

- 1 tablespoon extra-virgin olive oil
- 1 small white onion, diced
- 2 cloves garlic, minced
- ½ cup chick peas or garbanzo beans (about ½ can)
- 1 can diced tomatoes, drained (or 8 Roma tomatoes, diced)
- ½ teaspoon ground cumin
- 1 teaspoon cinnamon
- 2 teaspoons sweet paprika
- 2 cups red or Swiss chard, chopped
- 6 eggs
- Fresh basil or parsley for garnish
- Salt and pepper to taste

1. Preheat oven to 400°.

2. In an oven-proof medium skillet, heat extra-virgin olive oil over medium-high heat. Add onion and garlic and sauté for 5 minutes.

3. Add chick peas and sauté another 3 to 4 minutes.

4. Add tomatoes, cumin, cinnamon, and paprika. Bring to a boil. Lower heat and simmer 10 minutes.

5. Add chard and cook 1 to 2 minutes.

6. Remove from heat. Make small wells with the back of a spoon in the tomato and chard mixture. Add an egg carefully into each well.

7. Move skillet to the preheated oven and bake 15 to 20 minutes, until egg whites are set.

8. Remove from oven and cool slightly. Garnish with basil, parsley, or both. Add salt and pepper to taste.

9. Serve with toasted multigrain bread, semolina bread, toasted pita bread or triangles, or fluffy naan bread.

Pasta with Spinach, Tomato & Poached Egg

Pasta with Spinach, Tomato & Poached Egg

Eggs are one of the easiest, inexpensive sources of protein and can be used in so many ways. This is another simple recipe that provides protein, fiber, and lots of flavor. It's perfect for a weeknight meal, a brunch dish, or lunch with friends. Don't be put off by poaching the eggs. It's easier than you think! This recipe is delicious as leftovers and does double duty as lunch the next day or as a unique entrée for a party.

Makes 4 servings

- 8 ounces uncooked pasta (whole-wheat, gluten-free, or low-carb pasta is fine)
- 2 tablespoons extra-virgin olive oil
- 2 large (or 6 Roma) tomatoes, seeded and chopped into 1-inch pieces
- 1 garlic clove, minced
- Salt & pepper to taste
- 2 cups loosely packed baby spinach
- $1/2$ teaspoon paprika
- $1/2$ cup chopped fresh basil
- $1/4$ cup fresh-grated Parmesan cheese
- 1 tablespoon white vinegar
- 4 eggs

1. Cook pasta according to package directions and set aside.

2. In a large skillet over medium-high heat, heat extra-virgin olive oil. Add tomatoes, garlic, salt, and pepper. Cook, stirring often, until tomatoes are soft, about 8 to 10 minutes.

3. Add spinach and paprika. Cook, stirring occasionally, until spinach is wilted.

4. Add tomatoes and spinach mixture to pasta and toss to combine. Top with a poached egg, basil, and Parmesan cheese.

This is the easiest way to make a poached egg!!

If using the poached egg:

1. In a small, shallow skillet, bring 2 inches of water to a slow boil (e.g., bubbles at the corners but not the full rolling boil you use for making pasta).

2. Add white vinegar.

3. Carefully crack open each egg over a strainer or slotted spoon. Allow the thin egg white to drain off, leaving only the yolk and the thicker, dense egg white closest to the yolk.

4. Stir the water in a large circle 4 to 5 times to create a small whirlpool. Slowly add 1 egg at a time into the center of the whirlpool. Poach for 3 minutes.

5. Turn off the heat, remove from heat, and cover the pot until ready to use.

6. Remove 1 egg at a time, draining off or tapping off any excess water before placing onto the pasta.

Pea, Edamame & Farro Stir Fry

Pea, Edamame & Farro Stir Fry

This stir fry is easy, quick, and loaded with protein, nutrients, and flavor. Farro is an ancient grain that is loaded with flavor and nutrients, like fiber, protein, and essential vitamins and minerals, like vitamin B, zinc, and magnesium. Edamame is another nutrient-rich powerhouse loaded with protein (about 18 grams per cup), low in fat, and high in iron, fiber, calcium, and magnesium. The combination of farro, edamame, and peas adds up to one delicious, nutritious meal. This recipe can be customized any way you wish. Try adding more vegetables, nuts, tofu, or whatever spice you like.

Makes 4 servings

- 2 teaspoons extra-virgin olive oil, divided
- 1 large egg, beaten
- 1 small onion, thinly sliced
- 2 cloves garlic, minced
- Salt and pepper to taste
- ⅔ cup cooked farro
- 1 cup frozen peas, thawed and drained
- 1 cup frozen edamame, thawed and drained
- ½ cup julienned fresh basil
- ¼ teaspoon paprika

1. In a large skillet over medium-high heat, heat 1 teaspoon of extra-virgin olive oil. When oil is hot, add the egg, stirring constantly, until egg is cooked, about 30 seconds. Transfer to a plate and set aside.

2. Return the skillet to the heat and add remaining 1 teaspoon of extra-virgin olive oil. Add onion and cook until softened, about 4 to 5 minutes.

3. Add garlic, salt, and pepper and cook until fragrant, about 1 minute.

4. Add all remaining ingredients and cooked egg. Cook, stirring occasion-ally, until farro, peas, and edamame are heated through and thoroughly combined.

5. Serve in bowls. Sprinkle with crushed peanuts, diced green onion, chives, or finely chopped parsley.

Quick Edamame Salad

Quick Edamame Salad

Edamame are young soybeans that are high in protein, fiber, calcium, vitamin A and C, and, most importantly, iron. Though they're young soybeans, edamame do not contain high levels of phytoestrogens, like traditional soy products, so they become a great source of nutrition for an entire family.

Makes 4 servings

- 1 16-ounce package frozen shelled edamame, thawed
- 1 16-ounce package frozen sweet corn, thawed
- 1 12-ounce can black beans, drained and rinsed
- 1 16-ounce package frozen sweet peas, thawed
- ½ small red onion, finely minced
- ¼ cup extra-virgin olive oil
- ¼ cup red wine or balsamic vinegar
- Salt & pepper to taste
- ¼ teaspoon garlic powder
- 1 teaspoon fresh basil, chopped
- 1 teaspoon fresh parsley, chopped

1. Mix edamame, corn, beans, peas, and red onion in a large bowl.

2. Stir together extra-virgin olive oil, the vinegar, salt, pepper, garlic powder, basil, and parsley. Add to edamame mixture.

3. Chill in refrigerator for 30 to 60 minutes. Toss again prior to serving.

Quinoa & Black Bean Stuffed Acorn Squash

Quinoa & Black Bean Stuffed Acorn Squash

Acorn squash has a unique flavor of its own and an easy way to magnify and accent that flavor is to cook it then stuff it. Acorn squash has virtually no fat or sodium but is high in potassium, B vitamins, magnesium, and fiber. The yellow or orange pulp inside the squash is also high in antioxidants, beta-carotene, and vitamin C. Add in a healthy stuffing and squash can become a meal on its own. This recipe combines protein-packed beans, avocado, and quinoa into a delicious, savory stuffing for roasted acorn squash. The addition of finely diced zucchini takes the place of breadcrumbs and works to bind all the ingredients together, including the subtle spices.

Makes 2 servings

- Vegetable cooking spray
- 1 acorn squash halved, with seeds removed
- ½ cup uncooked quinoa
- 1 cup vegetable or chicken broth
- ¼ cup chopped cilantro or parsley, plus extra for garnish
- 1 tablespoon extra-virgin olive oil
- 1 medium green zucchini, finely diced
- 1 garlic clove, minced
- ⅛ teaspoon onion powder
- ⅛ teaspoon cumin
- 1 can black beans, rinsed and drained
- ½ avocado, diced

1. Preheat oven to 375°. Lightly grease a baking sheet.

2. Spray the prepared squash with vegetable oil spray. Place skin side down on baking sheet and cook until tender and skin separates easily from the flesh of the squash, about 35 to 40 minutes.

3. While the squash is baking, cook quinoa by combining broth and quinoa in a medium saucepan. Cook per package directions.

4. When quinoa is cooked, remove from heat and stir in cilantro or parsley. Set aside to cool.

5. In a medium skillet, heat extra-virgin olive oil over medium heat. Add in the diced zucchini and cook until slightly tender, 3 to 4 minutes.

6. Add in garlic, onion powder, and cumin. Cook 3 minutes, until zucchini is soft. Remove from heat.

7. In a large bowl, stir together the cooked quinoa, black beans, and zucchini mixture until combined.

8. Stuff each half of acorn squash with the quinoa, black bean, and vegetable mixture. Top with pieces of diced avocado and garnish with additional cilantro or parsley. Serve warm.

Ratatouille

Ratatouille

Ratatouille is a French stew from the Provencal region. It uses vegetables that are slowly cooked and blended together to create an incredible, hearty stew. The vegetables provide vitamins, minerals, fiber, and essential amino acids. The olive oil they're cooked in is a healthy fat. This dish, however, takes time to prep all the ingredients and then cook. Once prepared, ratatouille can be used in several ways. The results are worth the effort, and this makes a great dish.

Makes 6 to 8 servings

- 6 tablespoons extra-virgin olive oil, plus more for serving
- 1 large eggplant, cut into ⅓-inch cubes
- ¼ teaspoon salt, plus more to taste
- 2 medium zucchinis, cut into ⅓-inch cubes
- 1 medium onion, finely chopped
- 4 large cloves garlic, chopped
- 5 large tomatoes, cut into⅓-inch cubes, with their juices (or use 1 large [28 ounce] can peeled tomatoes with its juice or 1 pint of cherry tomatoes, halved)
- 1 tablespoon tomato paste
- 2 teaspoons fresh chopped thyme, plus more for serving
- ¾ teaspoon sugar
- 3 tablespoons chopped fresh basil

1. Heat 3 tablespoons of oil in a large nonstick pan over medium heat.

2. Add the eggplant and season with ¼ teaspoon salt. Cook, stirring frequently, until soft and starting to brown, 10 to 12 minutes. Transfer to a plate lined with paper towels and set aside.

3. Add another tablespoon of oil to the pan. Add the zucchini and cook,

stirring frequently, until tender-crisp, 3 to 4 minutes. Sprinkle with some salt and transfer to a second plate lined with paper towels (not the one with the eggplant—both get added separately).Keep it set aside.

4. Add two more tablespoons of oil to the pan and add the onion. Cook, stirring frequently, for about 5 minutes. Add the garlic and continue cooking for about 3 minutes more.

5. Add the tomatoes (and their juice), tomato paste, thyme, sugar, and another sprinkle of salt. Cook, stirring occasionally, until the tomatoes are broken down into a sauce, 8 to 10 minutes.

6. Add the cooked eggplant to the pan; bring to a gentle boil then reduce the heat to low and simmer, uncovered, for about 10 minutes or until the eggplant is soft.

7. Add the zucchini and cook for 1 to 2 minutes more, or until just warmed through.

8. Taste and adjust seasoning, if necessary.

9. Sprinkle with fresh basil and thyme and drizzle with a little olive oil if desired.

10. Serve warm or chilled. Leftovers can be stored in the refrigerator in an airtight container for up to 5 to 7 days or frozen for up to 2 months.

Succotash

Succotash

Succotash is super versatile as either a vegetarian dish or one with meat, and it can be loaded with healthy nutrition. The vegetables are typically full of vitamins and minerals, amino acids, potassium, and needed fiber. Succotash traditionally contains some form of corn and lima beans, but there are plenty of flavors that can be added into succotash to give it lots of extra flavor and color. While fresh ingredients are best, this dish can be made with frozen vegetables too. Different regions have used okra, beans, potatoes, or carrots. Try either the vegetarian version or the meat version for your next main course or side dish.

Makes 4 to 6 servings

- 2 tablespoons extra-virgin olive oil
- 1 onion, diced small
- 2 cloves of garlic, smashed
- 5 ears of corn, husks removed, and kernels cut off (do not cook!) or 1 large bag of frozen yellow corn, thawed
- Salt to taste
- 1 pint of cherry tomatoes, halved
- Pepper to taste
- 1 box (or small bag) of frozen lima beans, thawed
- ½ cup frozen peas

1. In a large, heavy skillet heat extra-virgin olive oil over medium heat.

2. Add onion and cook until onions are translucent, about 5 to 6 minutes. Add garlic and cook 1 minute until fragrant

3. Add in the corn, sprinkle with salt, and cover. Continue cooking over medium heat until corn is cooked, 5 minutes.

4. Add in tomatoes, sprinkle with salt and pepper, and continue cooking for 3 to 4 minutes.

5. Add in lima beans and cook an additional 4 minutes or until lima beans are softened.

6. Add in peas and cover, cooking an additional 2 to 3 minutes, until peas turn bright green and are heated through.

Succotash with Meat

Makes 4 to 6 servings

- 1 tablespoon extra-virgin olive oil
- 1 tablespoon unsalted butter
- 3 slices of bacon, diced
- 1 onion, diced small
- 2 cloves of garlic, smashed
- 5 ears of corn, husks removed, and kernels cut off (do not cook!) or 1 large bag of frozen yellow corn, thawed
- Salt to taste
- 1 pint of cherry tomatoes, halved
- Pepper to taste
- 1 box (or small bag) of frozen lima beans, thawed
- ½ cup frozen peas

1. In a large, heavy skillet heat extra-virgin olive oil and butter over medium heat.

2. Add the bacon and cook until the fat is rendered and the bacon pieces are crisp, about 4 to 5 minutes.

3. Remove the bacon pieces and drain on a plate with paper towels.

4. Add onion to the oil/butter/bacon fat and cook until onions are translu-cent, about 5 to 6 minutes. Add garlic and cook until fragrant, about 1 minute.

5. Add in the corn, sprinkle with salt, and cover. Continue cooking over medium heat until corn is cooked, 5 minutes.

6. Add in tomatoes, sprinkle with salt and pepper, and continue cooking for 3 to 4 minutes.

7. Add in lima beans and cook an additional 4 minutes or until lima beans are softened.

8. Add in peas and cover, cooking an additional 2 to 3 minutes, until peas turn bright green and are heated through.

9. Add the bacon pieces back into the succotash and toss to combine.

Vegetable Pasta Toss

Vegetable Pasta Toss

This pasta toss is one more example of a quick and easy meal that comes together in no time and tastes delicious. This recipe can be changed up any way you like, including using different vegetables, pasta, or cheeses. Frozen or fresh vegetables work well in this recipe so feel free to clean out the freezer and use whatever you have on hand to create new flavor combinations.

Makes 4 to 6 servings

- 2 medium zucchinis, shaved or peeled into long ribbons (or use a vegetable spiralizer to make noodles)
- Salt to taste
- 1 8-ounce package of pappardelle or tagliatelle pasta
- ½ pound fresh green beans trimmed and cut into 2-inch pieces (or 2 cups frozen cut green beans, thawed)
- 4 to 5 stalks asparagus, sliced diagonally
- 1 cup cherry tomatoes, halved
- ½ cup part-skim Ricotta cheese
- Pepper to taste
- ¼ cup grated Pecorino Romano cheese
- ¼ cup chopped fresh parsley

1. Add zucchini to a colander and sprinkle lightly with salt. Allow to sit 10 to 15 minutes to drain some of the excess liquid.

2. Bring a 5- to 6-quart pot filled with cold water to a boil. Cook pasta according to the package directions until al dente. Add green beans and asparagus during last minute of cooking. Reserve 1 cup of pasta water.

3. Drain pasta, green beans, and asparagus over the zucchini in the colander.

4. Return pasta and vegetable mix to the pot. Add in tomatoes and stir.

5. Add Ricotta cheese, salt, pepper, and ½ cup of reserved pasta water and stir to combine. Add more pasta water, 1 tablespoon at a time as needed, until cheese sauce is desired consistency.

6. Divide pasta mixture into serving bowls. Garnish with sprinkles of Pecorino Romano and parsley. Serve with fresh green salad or toasted pieces of multigrain bread.

Vegetable Spring Rolls

Vegetable Spring Rolls

This recipe is the foundation for you to make your own Asian-inspired spring rolls. Everyone will love that these spring rolls are low in carbs, sugar, and sodium. Make these spring rolls as an easy lunch, simple appetizer, or a light dinner. Most grocery stores and supermarkets already have most of the ingredients pre-cut so feel free to take advantage of any convenience you find. You can change them up by simply changing the ingredients: try shrimp, avocado, seasonal fruits, micro greens, chopped chicken, fish, pork, or different herbs.

Makes 8-10 spring rolls

- 1 package of vermicelli-style rice noodles or thin rice noodles
- 1/2 cup chopped cilantro or parsley
- 1/2 cup chopped basil
- 1/2 cup chopped mint
- 1 package rice roll wrappers
- 1 large carrot, peeled and cut into thin strips
- 1 cucumber, peeled and cut into thin strips
- 1 small head of red cabbage, shredded or cut into thin strips
- Optional: shrimp or meat filling
- Optional: 1 mango or 1/2 pineapple cut into thin strips

1. Cook rice noodles in boiling water according to package directions. Drain noodles after cooking and rinse with cold water. Set aside.

2. Prepare all ingredients in advance. Mix the herbs together in one medium-sized bowl.

3. Fill a 9-inch pie plate with 1 to 2 inches of cold water. Place 1 rice wrapper in the water and soak for only 10 to 20 seconds. It should still be firm and not tear when handled when removing from the water.

4. With the rice wrapper on a flat, nonstick surface (or a surface lined with wax paper or plastic wrap), layer 2 to 3 slices of each vegetable, shrimp, or meat filling, if using, small pinches of the herb mixture, and a small pinch of the cooled rice noodles on the ⅓ of the wrapper closest to you.

5. Fold the sides of the spring roll in over the ingredients. Pull the side closest to you up and over the ingredients (it will now overlap the 2 folded sides). Roll the wrapper away from you to seal in the ingredients.

6. Each roll can be wrapped individually to keep them fresh or use wax paper between them to prevent them from sticking. Store in an airtight container.

Option: These spring rolls can be served hot too! Bring 2 to 3 inches of water to a boil in a wide pot or skillet.Using a wire or steam basket, steam 2 or 3 rolls at a time for 2 to 5 minutes, until the wrapper is translucent. Remove from heat and serve with Peanut Dipping Sauce (see the recipe for Peanut Chicken in Lettuce Cups) or with Sweet Chili sauce.

Veggie Cakes

Veggie Cakes

These super-easy vegetable cakes satisfy hunger and provide energy. These cakes are loaded with good stuff: vegetables, some needed carbs, lots of flavor, and texture. They can be used as a lunch, a light dinner, or a snack. These cakes work for the whole family: they are perfect for anyone and can also do double duty as a party meal, hors d'oeuvres, or even as a side dish to a roasted meat or on top of salad. These cakes can be made in any size so they can serve as an entrée or a perfect appetizer. Change up the type of vegetables used or experiment with different dipping sauces.

Makes 12 cakes

- 2 medium zucchinis, grated and drained
- 1 teaspoon salt
- 1 cup grated broccoli (about 1 or 2 stems and heads)
- 3 carrots, grated
- 1 cup frozen yellow corn, thawed and drained
- 2 green onions, finely diced
- $1/2$ cup all-purpose flour (or whole-wheat flour)
- $1/2$ teaspoon baking powder
- $1/2$ cup Panko breadcrumbs
- $1/2$ cup fresh-grated Parmesan cheese (optional)
- 3 eggs
- $1/2$ teaspoon black pepper
- 2 tablespoons extra-virgin olive oil

1. Place grated zucchini into a colander or strainer and add salt. Cover with a paper towel and weight down (e.g., with a can of tomatoes or another heavy kitchen item). Allow to sit and drain for 30 minutes to 1 hour.

2. In a food processor, pulse broccoli and carrots into smaller pieces. Add to a large mixing bowl.

3. After the zucchini has drained, wrap in a kitchen towel or bundle of paper towels and squeeze out as much liquid as possible. Rewrap often and squeeze immediately until no more liquid comes out.

4. Add zucchini to broccoli and carrots. Add corn and green onions.

5. In a medium bowl, mix flour, baking powder, Panko breadcrumbs, and cheese, if using.

6. Add flour mixture to the vegetable mixture and toss thoroughly to coat each piece of vegetable with flour mixture.

7. In a small bowl, whisk eggs and pepper slightly. Pour over vegetable and flour mixture and stir to combine.

8. In a medium nonstick skillet over medium-high heat, heat extra-virgin olive oil.

9. Using an ice cream scooper or large spoon, spoon ½ cup of vegetable mixture and form into patties. Drop into heated oil and flatten slightly to create an even cooking surface.

10. Cook 3 to 4 minutes on each side until golden brown, careful not to burn either side.

11. Remove cooked cake to a cooling rack or on paper towels and allow to cool. Cook additional cakes in similar batches.

12. Serve warm with a fresh salad, fruit, quinoa, rice, or steamed edamame. Store in refrigerator for up to 3 days and reheat as needed or freeze in an airtight container for up to 2 months.

Veggie Sticks

Veggie Sticks

These veggie sticks are super easy to make and a few simple add-ins or toppings easily elevate the flavor to the next level. Try different herbs, cheeses, or dipping sauces—you can't go wrong. These can be made in larger batches so they're on hand whenever you're craving a snack. Cut the vegetables into spears or wedges. They cook at a high temperature, so they become crispy on the outside and tender on the inside. Make different batches then use different vegetable combinations for even more flavor. Root vegetables work best, but the base recipe is the same for any vegetable used, so feel free to experiment with whatever kind of vegetables you like.

Makes 2 to 4 servings

- 1 pound of a sturdy root vegetable (carrots, parsnips, beets, jicamas, potatoes, or sweet potatoes), peeled and cut into ½-inch spears or wedges
- 1 tablespoon extra-virgin olive oil
- ½ teaspoon salt

1. Preheat oven to 425°. Line a baking sheet with parchment paper.

2. In a large bowl, toss the cut pieces of vegetables with the extra-virgin olive oil and salt until all pieces of vegetables are coated with the oil and salt mixture.

3. Spread the vegetables in a single layer on the prepared baking sheet.

4. Cook 20 to 25 minutes. Remove from the oven and allow to cool 2 to 4 minutes then sprinkle with any desired toppings.

Optional Seasonings and Toppings

Beets: sprinkle with ¼ cup fresh-grated Parmesan cheese after cooking.

Parsnips: toss with 1 tablespoon chopped fresh rosemary before cooking.

Carrots: toss with 1 tablespoon of curry powder, cinnamon, or ¼ teaspoon Sriracha sauce before cooking.

Jicama: toss with ½ teaspoon ground cumin or sweet paprika before cooking.

White Bean Salad with Chicken

White Bean Salad with Chicken

A salad can be loaded with taste, protein, and other healthy nutrients by using simple things you may already have on hand. This White Bean Salad with Chicken can be served warm or cold. You can add in as many ingredients as you like or use more of ones that are your favorites without changing how healthy it is. Typically served with a zesty vinaigrette, any type of dressing can be used. This salad can be used as a side dish to your favorite piece of roasted meat or fish. Try experimenting with different ingredient combinations but be sure to keep the beans for protein and fiber.

Makes 4 to 6 servings

Vinaigrette

- 1 clove garlic, finely minced
- 5 tablespoons extra-virgin olive oil
- 5-6 tablespoons fresh squeezed orange juice
- ¼ cup red or white wine vinegar
- 1 tablespoon Dijon or brown mustard
- ¼ teaspoon salt

Salad

- 1 15-ounce can of white cannellini beans, rinsed and drained
- 2 cups diced, cooked chicken
- 2 cups diced zucchini
- 1 cup diced celery
- ½ cup diced sun-dried tomatoes in oil, drained
- ¼ cup finely diced feta cheese
- 1 cup diced, fresh basil
- Salt and pepper to taste
- 2 cups chopped arugula, escarole, romaine, or Bibb lettuce

278

1. Prepare vinaigrette: Put finely minced garlic in a small bowl. Whisk in extra-virgin olive oil. Add orange juice, vinegar, and mustard; whisk until blended. Season with salt and pepper. Add in additional orange juice and salt and pepper as needed for taste. Set aside.

2. Prepare the salad: Combine beans, chicken, zucchini, celery, and sun-dried tomatoes in a large bowl. Add in feta cheese, basil, and vinaigrette; toss gently to coat. Season with salt and pepper to taste.

3. Place greens on a plate and spoon the salad on top. Or gently toss greens with salad mix and serve in a bowl garnished with additional basil.

Hint: Do not mix greens with salad mixture if not eating immediately. The vinaigrette will wilt the greens and make them soggy. Instead, wrap the greens in damp paper towels and keep in a plastic bag in the refrigerator until ready to serve.

Wild Rice & Edamame Salad

Wild Rice & Edamame Salad

This is the perfect side dish or as a meal on its own! It's loaded with protein and fiber from the edamame, has a nutty flavor from the wild rice, and the slightest touch of sweetness from the carrots, cranberries, and rice vinegar. Plus, it's fast and easy!

Makes 4 to 6 servings

- ¼ cup blanched, slivered almonds
- 1 tablespoon white sesame seeds
- 2 cups cooked wild rice, cooled
- 2 scallions, thin sliced (green parts only)
- 1 cup frozen edamame, thawed
- 1 medium carrot, peeled and diced small
- ¼ cup dried cranberries
- ½ cup extra-virgin olive oil
- 2 teaspoons toasted sesame oil
- ¼ cup rice vinegar
- 1–2 teaspoons honey
- Salt & pepper to taste

1. Prepare the almonds: In a medium frying pan, over medium heat, toast the almonds, stirring often, until the almonds are golden brown and fragrant, approximately 8 minutes. Transfer to a bowl and cool.

2. Add sesame seeds and toast, stirring often, until golden brown, approximately 2 to 3 minutes. Add to the bowl with the almonds.

3. Add wild rice, scallions, edamame, carrot, and cranberries to bowl with almonds and sesame seeds. Toss to combine.

4. In a small bowl, whisk extra-virgin olive oil, sesame oil, rice vinegar, honey, and pinches of salt and pepper until combined.

5. Drizzle oil mixture over rice mixture and toss to combine. Season with additional salt and pepper to taste.

6. Cover and chill for 1 to 2 hours before serving.

This recipe can be doubled. This dish stores well—just toss again prior to serving.

VI

Desserts

Best Brownies

Best Brownies

Brownies are the ultimate chocolate comfort food! These brownies will become your next go-to favorite. They're super simple to make and can be mixed all in one bowl. You can make them moist and fudgy or more cake-like just by changing the length of time you bake them (i.e., cook less for more fudge-like brownies and longer for more cake-like texture). These brownies use Greek yogurt to keep them moist and substitute Stevia for regular white sugar. These brownies can be cut into small snack-size pieces and stored for up to 1 week in an airtight container in the refrigerator or freezer for up to one month. Try using different types of chocolate or add in different flavors like raisins, cranberries, nuts, or seeds or use them as toppings.

Makes 16 brownies

- 1 tablespoon unsalted butter, melted and slightly cooled
- 2 egg whites
- 1 teaspoon vanilla
- Pinch of salt
- ¼ cup nonfat plain Greek yogurt
- ¼ cup Stevia
- 5 tablespoons milk (nonfat, low-fat or 2%)
- ¾ cup unsweetened cocoa powder
- ¼ teaspoon baking powder
- ¾ cup whole-wheat flour
- 2 tablespoons chopped dark chocolate

1. Preheat oven to 300°. Lightly coat an 8x8-inch baking dish with vegetable spray or use overlapping pieces of parchment paper to line the baking dish.

2. In a large bowl, whisk the butter, egg whites, vanilla, and salt until combined.

3. Stir in Greek yogurt and mix well.

4. Stir in the Stevia and milk and mix well.

5. Add in the cocoa powder and baking powder and mix well.

6. Stir in the flour until combined. Do not over mix. Fold in the chopped chocolate.

7. Spread the batter evenly in the prepared baking dish.

8. Bake 15 to 20 minutes, depending on which texture you prefer for the brownies.

9. Remove from the oven and allow to cool completely on a wire rack. Slice when cooled into squares.

Better Chocolate Chip Cookies

Better Chocolate Chip Cookies

This recipe allows everyone to enjoy the flavors, textures, and comfort of a classic favorite with some better ingredients, compared to the classic recipe. Change up the fruit, nuts, or type of chocolate to create different flavor combinations and profiles.

Makes 12 to 14 cookies

- ½ cup unsalted butter
- ⅓ cup granulated sugar
- ⅓ cup light brown sugar, packed
- ¼ teaspoon salt
- ¼ teaspoon baking soda
- ¼ teaspoon baking powder
- 1 teaspoon vanilla extract
- 1 egg
- ¾ cup whole-wheat flour
- 1 cup rolled oats (or ¾ cup oat flour)
- 2 cups chocolate chips
- Optional: 1 cup chopped nuts, 1 cup chocolate carob chips, or 1 cup dried fruit

1. Preheat oven to 375°. Line 2 baking sheets with parchment paper.

2. Beat together butter, sugars, salt, baking soda, baking powder, and vanilla extract until combined and smooth.

3. Add egg and beat until smooth. Scrapes the sides of the bowl frequently to incorporate all ingredients.

4. Add in the flour and the oats. Stir to combine. Add in the chips and/or other add-ins. Stir to combine.

5. Drop dough in 1-inch balls onto a parchment-lined baking sheet. Bake 10 to 15 minutes, until cookies are golden brown.

6. Cool 1 to 3 minutes. Remove cookies to a wire rack and cool completely. Store in an airtight container or freeze up to 2 months.

Blueberry Coffee Cake

Blueberry Coffee Cake

Fresh blueberries are the hallmark of this recipe. Blueberries have a natural sweetness that decreases the need for lots of added sugar. In addition, the blueberries add in essential vitamins, fiber, and powerful antioxidants. The addition of whole-wheat flour adds a delicious earthy taste, and the use of spices, nuts, and Greek yogurt provides different textures and incredible taste. Feel free to use chopped almonds or finely chopped hazelnuts—you can't go wrong. The possibilities are endless!

Makes 12 servings

- ¾ cup all-purpose flour
- ¾ cup whole-wheat flour
- 1 teaspoon baking soda
- 1 teaspoon baking powder
- ½ teaspoon salt
- 2 tablespoons granulated sugar
- ½ teaspoon ground cinnamon
- ½ cup chopped walnuts (optional)
- ½ cup light brown sugar, packed
- 2 tablespoons butter, softened
- 2 tablespoons light olive oil or light vegetable oil
- 2 eggs
- 1 teaspoon vanilla
- ¾ cup plain Greek yogurt
- 1 cup blueberries, fresh or frozen and thawed
- 1 teaspoon fresh lemon zest

1. Preheat oven to 350°. Spray an 8-inch square or 9-inch round springform pan with vegetable spray.

2. Whisk flours, baking soda, baking powder, and salt in a medium bowl. Set aside.

3. In a small bowl, combine granulated sugar, cinnamon, and nuts if using. Set aside.

4. In a large bowl, beat brown sugar, butter, and olive oil until fluffy and combined. Beat in 1 egg at a time until combined. Beat in vanilla and yogurt.

5. Add flour mixture in spoonfuls to sugar and butter mixture. Stir in blueberries and lemon zest.

6. Spread half the batter into the prepared pan. Sprinkle half the sugar/cinnamon and nut mixture over the batter. Spoon in the remaining batter. Top with remaining sugar/cinnamon and nut mixture.

7. Bake 30 to 35 minutes, until a toothpick inserted in the center comes out clean.

8. Cool slightly then remove from pan to cool completely. Cut into individual servings. Wrap each piece individually in plastic wrap and keep in the refrigerator for up to 1 week or wrap cake tightly in plastic wrap and freeze for up to 2 weeks

Broiled or Grilled Bananas

Broiled or Grilled Bananas

Bananas are high in fiber, potassium, magnesium, vitamin B6, folate, and vitamin C. This recipe is a way to maximize the natural sweetness or sugars in bananas and still extract all the health benefits from this versatile fruit. This recipe is super easy to prepare and tastes delicious with a variety of toppings, like Greek yogurt, granola, chopped nuts, or even sweet herbs, like finely diced tarragon or rosemary. Try fresh whipped cream, sorbet, chilled pineapple, or homemade vanilla ice cream too.

Makes 2 to 4 servings

- · 2 ripe bananas
- · 1 tablespoon brown sugar
- · 1 tablespoon lemon juice
- · Optional: frozen yogurt, ice cream, fresh whipped cream, Greek yogurt, honey, granola, chopped nuts, or a sprinkle of cinnamon or cardamom

To broil

1. Preheat Broiler.

2. Peel bananas and slice crosswise into ¾-inch thick slices.

3. Mix brown sugar and lemon juice in a small bowl and toss with bananas.

4. Spread the coated banana slices in a shallow baking dish or on a sheet pan.

5. Broil as close to the heat source as possible until the sugar melts into a glaze, approximately 2 to 3 minutes.

6. Serve immediately and top with Greek yogurt, honey, cinnamon, granola, sliced almonds or other nuts, fresh whipped cream, or ice cream.

To grill

1. Spray a grill pan or outdoor grill with vegetable spray. Heat over medium heat.

2. Peel bananas and slice crosswise into ¾-inch thick slices.

3. Mix brown sugar and lemon juice in a small bowl and toss with banana slices.

4. Spread the coated banana slices on center of grill.

5. Grill for 2 minutes or until grill marks appear, approximately 2 to 2 ½ minutes each side. Be careful not to have heat too high or bananas will stick.

6. Remove from heat and serve immediately.

Top or garnish with frozen yogurt, ice cream, fresh whipped cream, Greek yogurt, honey, granola, chopped nuts, or a sprinkle of cinnamon or cardamom.

Chewy Oatmeal Cookies

Chewy Oatmeal Cookies

These oatmeal cookies are full of healthy fiber from the oats and the whole-wheat flour that will keep hunger at bay. Instead of lots of sugar, this recipe combines natural honey with the sweetness of raisins to bring about incredible taste. This recipe is also lower in fat than most traditional cookies. The secret to this recipe is to allow ample time for the dough to chill so they're easy to drop onto a baking sheet. When they're done cooking, give them enough time to cool completely. Try swapping out the raisins for dried cranberries, cherries, blueberries, yellow raisins, or even diced pieces of dried apricot or peaches.

Makes 15-16 cookies

- 1¼ cup rolled oats
- ¾ cup whole-wheat flour
- 1½ teaspoons baking powder
- 1½ teaspoons cinnamon
- Pinch of salt
- 2 tablespoons unsalted butter, melted and slightly cooled
- 1 large egg
- 1 teaspoon vanilla extract
- ½ cup natural honey
- ½ cup raisins

1. In a medium bowl, whisk the oats, whole-wheat flour, baking powder, cinnamon, and salt.

2. In a large bowl, whisk butter, egg, and vanilla until smooth. Stir in the honey and mix well to combine.

3. Add the flour mixture to the egg and honey mixture and stir until incorporated. Fold in the raisins. Cover with plastic wrap and refrigerate 30 to 45 minutes to chill the dough.

4. Preheat oven to 325°. Line a baking sheet with parchment paper.

5. Drop the chilled cookie dough in rounded tablespoons onto the prepared baking sheet.

6. Bake 11 to 14 minutes, until the cookies are browned. Remove from the oven and cool on a baking sheet for 10 minutes. Remove cookies to a wire rack and allow to cool completely.

Chia Seed Pudding

Chia Seed Pudding

Chia seeds are little powerhouses that contain the right amount of protein, fat, and fiber. This recipe is not only delicious but also useful as an energy boost any time of the day.

Makes 2 to 4 servings

- 1½ cup unsweetened almond milk
- ⅓ cup chia seeds
- ½ teaspoon vanilla
- ½ teaspoon cinnamon
- ¼ teaspoon salt
- 2-5 tablespoons of maple syrup (or agave syrup)

1. Add all ingredients together (except for syrup) and whisk vigorously.

2. Sweeten to your liking by adding a tablespoon of syrup at a time.

3. Pour into individual pudding cups or ramekins.

4. Refrigerate, covered, for at least 3 to 5 hours (overnight is best) until the mixture takes on a pudding-like consistency. Keeps well in the refrigerator for up to 3 days. For added taste, top with homemade granola or fresh fruit.

Dave's Cheesecake

Dave's Cheesecake

My partner, Dave, has one of the easiest recipes for a cheesecake that has become my family's (especially my mother's!) favorite recipe. Dave's cheesecake has simple ingredients that many of us have in our pantries. The flavor is subtle, but the texture is smooth, creamy, and rich. This recipe takes no time to make. There is no way to go wrong with this recipe, and it's perfect for people who aren't that comfortable baking or cooking and need a quick, easy, tasty dessert. It requires no baking and can be made well in advance.

Makes 8 servings

- 1 cup of fruit for the bottom: fresh blueberries, hulled and sliced fresh strawberries, pitted cherries, or sliced bananas (alone or a combination of fruit)
- 1 8-ounce package of low, reduced, or no-fat cream cheese, softened
- ¾ cup lemon juice (fresh squeezed or pre-packaged)
- 1 teaspoon vanilla or almond extract
- 1 can low-fat sweetened condensed milk

1. Line the bottom of a clean, dry 8- or 9-inch pie pan with the fruit or fruits of your choice. Overlap fruit pieces if necessary. Set aside.

2. In a large mixing bowl or in the bowl of a stand-up mixer, add the cream cheese, lemon juice, vanilla, and sweetened condensed milk. Beat on medium speed, scraping the sides often, until the ingredients are well incorporated.

3. Pour the cream cheese mixture over the fruit on the bottom of the pie pan.

4. Cover with plastic wrap and refrigerate for at least 8 hours or overnight, if possible.

5. Slice and serve with a garnish of additional fruit or a sprig of mint.

Easy Banana Pudding

Easy Banana Pudding

This Banana Pudding is easy to prepare and free of milk, fat, and gluten. It's low in sodium and sugar yet high in fiber, especially since the bananas in this recipe are sliced so they're easy to prepare. The almond milk is a unique twist that adds a nutty flavor to highlight the bananas and keep the pudding creamy. Try adding more bananas or sprinkle with a variety of toppings like fresh whipped cream, Greek yogurt, diced walnuts, a dusting of cocoa powder, or even some mini chocolate chips.

Makes 4 to 6 servings

- 3 egg yolks
- ½ cup sugar, divided
- 5 tablespoons flour or oat flour
- ½ teaspoon salt
- ½ teaspoon grated nutmeg
- 2½ cups unsweetened almond milk
- ½ teaspoon vanilla extract
- ½ teaspoon almond extract
- 3 bananas, sliced (slightly ripe bananas are best)
- Optional: fresh whipped cream, Greek yogurt, diced walnuts, a dusting of cocoa powder, or mini chocolate chips

1. In a medium bowl, beat egg yolks with ¼ cup sugar until creamy. Set aside.

2. In a medium saucepan, combine remaining ¼ cup sugar with flour, salt, and nutmeg. Add almond milk and cook over medium heat, stirring constantly until mixture thickens, approximately 7 to 8 minutes.

3. Add 3 to 4 tablespoons of the egg and sugar mixture slowly into the flour and almond milk mixture to temper. Add the remaining egg mixture into

the saucepan and cook, stirring constantly, for 2 minutes over medium heat. Remove from heat and allow to cool at room temperature.

4. When cooled, add vanilla and almond extracts until thoroughly combined.

5. Prepare the pudding: in a decorative glass, serving dish, glass bowl, or individual ramekin, Layer pudding mixture and sliced bananas alternatively, ending with a layer of pudding mixture.

6. Chill and refrigerate at least one hour. Garnish with fresh whipped cream, Greek yogurt, diced walnuts, a dusting of cocoa powder, or mini chocolate chips.

Easy Mango Sorbet

Easy Mango Sorbet

Mango is a versatile flavor that pairs very well with so many other different fruit flavors like raspberry, peach, blueberry, lime, or watermelon. It also goes well with smooth flavors like vanilla, lemon, or orange. This recipe is so easy to make, and a food processor makes it even easier to create. The simple syrup makes the sorbet smooth without any overpowering sweetness. The small amount of corn syrup, if using, helps reduce the ice crystals that can form when freezing to keep this sorbet soft or creamy.

Makes 4 servings

- 1 cup granulated sugar
- 1 cup water
- 3 cups frozen mango (either use packaged frozen mango in chunks or fresh mango peeled, diced, and frozen 2 to 2 ½ hours)
- 3 tablespoons fresh lime juice
- Optional: ¼ cup coconut milk
- 1-2 tablespoons light corn syrup

1. Make simple syrup: In a medium saucepan, combine sugar and water. Bring to a boil, stirring frequently until sugar has dissolved. Allow to cool.

2. In a food processor, combine mango,cooled simple syrup, and lime juice. Pulse or blend until the mix is smooth.

3. For creamier sorbet, add coconut milk and pulse 2 to 5 more times until desired consistency is reached.

4. To prevent ice crystals, stir in 1 to 2 tablespoons of light corn syrup and pulse until combined.

5. Freeze at least 3 hours until sorbet is firm and formed. Serve with fresh fruit, additional sprinkle of fresh lime juice, fresh whipped cream, orange wedges, raspberry sauce, sliced peaches, orange slices, a sprinkle of orange zest, or simple shortbread crackers or cookies.

"Flu Fighter" Cookies

"Flu Fighter" Cookies

These cookies contain several seasonings and ingredients that, in combination, work to provide some needed calories, fiber, and protein. When combined, these flavors aren't overpowering and may actually stimulate the appetite. These cookies can be eaten with a cup of tea or a glass of milk or juice. They can also be made in advance and stored in the freezer for several weeks or in an airtight container for several days. Make a batch of these early in the season and keep them on hand "just in case."

Makes 16 to 18 cookies

- 2¼ cups all-purpose flour
- 1¼ teaspoon baking powder
- ¾ teaspoon baking soda
- ¾ teaspoon ground cinnamon
- ½ teaspoon ground nutmeg
- Pinch ground cloves
- ¼ teaspoon salt
- 1 stick unsalted butter, softened
- 1 cup packed brown sugar
- 2 large eggs
- ¼ cup molasses
- ¼ cup plain Greek yogurt
- 1 tablespoon fresh grated ginger
- 2 teaspoons orange zest, finely grated
- ½ cup old-fashioned oats (not the quick-cooking kind)
- 1¼ cups golden raisins
- 1¼ cups dried cranberries
- ½ cup chopped walnuts (optional)
- ½ cup chopped almonds (optional)

1. Preheat oven to 375°.

2. Line 2 baking sheets with parchment paper.

3. In a medium bowl, whisk flour, baking powder, baking soda, cinnamon, nutmeg, cloves, and salt. Set aside.

4. In a large bowl, beat butter and brown sugar on medium speed with handheld or upright mixer until light and fluffy, about 3 to 4 minutes.

5. Beat in eggs, one at a time, fully incorporating each before adding the next.

6. Add molasses, yogurt, ginger, and orange zest and beat until smooth, scraping the sides of the bowl occasionally.

7. Change mixer to low speed and slowly add in flour mixture. Do not over mix or batter will be too sticky.

8. Fold in oats and half each of the raisins, cranberries, walnuts, and almonds, if using.

9. In a small bowl, stir together remaining raisins, cranberries, and almonds, if using, and set aside for a topping.

10. Drop heaping tablespoons of cookie dough onto the parchment-lined baking sheets. Top with a sprinkle of the dried fruit and nut mixture. Chill the trays for 30 minutes in the refrigerator.

11. After the cookie dough has set, bake until cookie is a dark, golden color but still soft, 10 to 12 minutes. Cool completely on a rack.

Healthier Lemon Cake

Healthier Lemon Cake

This cake is moist and creamy, yet lower in saturated fat and sugar but still has the same amazing flavor, texture, and moistness of a traditional pound cake. This recipe uses Greek yogurt that provides some extra protein and velvety texture to the cake that regular butter cannot. Like traditional pound cake, this cake can be used in a variety of other recipes like trifles, shortcakes, or ice cream desserts or it can be grilled, drizzled with chocolate, paired with fresh fruit, or dipped in fondue.

Makes 8 servings

- ¼ cup plain Greek yogurt (or vanilla or honey-flavored)
- Zest of 1 lemon
- ½ cup fresh-squeezed lemon juice
- 3¼ tablespoons olive or vegetable oil (or add in same amount of unsweetened apple sauce or additional Greek yogurt)
- ½ teaspoon vanilla extract
- 1 cup all-purpose flour
- ½ teaspoon baking soda
- ¼ teaspoon salt
- ½ cup sugar

Glaze

- ¼ cup powdered sugar
- 1 teaspoon fresh lemon juice or water

1. Preheat oven to 350°. Grease or use vegetable spray on an 8x5-inch loaf pan.

2. In a medium bowl, whisk yogurt, lemon zest, lemon juice, oil (or apple-sauce or additional yogurt, if using), and vanilla extract until combined.

3. In a second bowl, whisk flour, baking soda, salt, and sugar until combined.

4. Pour yogurt mixture into flour mixture gradually, stirring after each addition until combined and mixture isn't lumpy.

5. Pour cake mixture into loaf pan and bake for 25 minutes, until top is golden brown and a toothpick inserted in the center comes out clean. Remove from oven and allow to cool 20 to 25 minutes.

6. After cake cools, remove from loaf pan and invert. Allow to cool completely.

7. Mix glaze. Use additional lemon juice or water until desired consistency. Spread glaze evenly over the top of the cake, allowing it to drip down the sides. Glaze will harden as it cools.

8. Store cake in a cool, dry place, Refrigerate or freeze if needed. Serve in 1-2-inch slices, with additional fruit or fresh whipped cream alongside a cup of herbal tea.

Heavenly Angel Food Cake

Heavenly Angel Food Cake

Because this cake contains no egg yolks, butter, or oil, its low in fat and low in carbohydrates. Since most of the cake batter is made with egg whites, it's also one of the few desserts that is high in protein (about 28 grams). It pairs with almost any fruit, especially with different mixtures of berries, peaches, plums, bananas, shaved coconut, or dried fruits. It's also perfect on its own or drizzled lightly with maple syrup, natural honey, or a dash of powdered sugar.

Some people are leery about making an angel food cake because they think it's too hard. Here are some tips to making the perfect angel food cake:

- Make sure the mixing bowl is clean, dry and has no traces of oil or grease that could deflate the egg whites.
- Carefully measure out the sugar- too much sugar prevents the cake from rising or causes it to fall.
- Use cake flour if possible. If not, you can create cake flour by combining all-purpose flour with 3 tablespoons of corn starch and pulsing in the food processor a few times.
- Use superfine sugar if possible. If not, white sugar can be pulsed a few times in the food processor to make it fine.
- Use only a simple tube pan. Do not use a Bundt pan because it has too many crevices and corners that prevent the cake from cooking evenly.
- Do not grease the tube pan.
- Invert the tube pan when the cake comes out of the oven and let it cool upside down (I promise the cake will not fall out!)

Makes 8-10 servings

- 1 1/3 cups cake flour
- 1¼ cups superfine sugar, divided
- 2 cups egg whites (about 12 to 16 large eggs)

- ½ teaspoon salt
- 1 teaspoon vanilla

1. Preheat oven to 350°. Use a tube pan and be sure the center is clean and dry.

2. Sift the cake flour and ½ cup superfine sugar together.

3. In a stand-up mixer with the whisk attachment (or in a large bowl with an electric mixer and the whisk blades attached), whip the egg whites on low speed until they become foamy. As the egg mixture begins to stiffen, gradually increase the mixer speed. Add in the salt and vanilla.

4. Gradually add in the remaining ¾ cup superfine sugar and continue to whip the egg whites until medium peaks form.

5. Gradually fold in increments of the flour mixture, turning carefully after each addition to not deflate the batter. Bake 40 to 45 minutes, until the cake springs back when lightly touched. Remove from the oven.

6. Carefully invert the tube pan (either on its own legs or set and balance the tube portion of the pan onto small unopened can like a soup can) and let it cool inverted for up to 1 hour. Use a knife along the edges to gently loosen the cake from the pan before removing.

7. Cool cake completely on a wire rack or cake stand. Serve with your choice of whipped topping, mixed berries, fresh fruit, natural honey, maple syrup, or a dusting of powdered sugar.

Marbled Banana Bread

Marbled Banana Bread

Banana bread on its own is delicious, but often it's loaded with sugars or fats. This recipe uses a ribbon of dark chocolate to balance out the sweetness of the cake and some buttermilk for texture. Don't have buttermilk on hand? No problem. Simply mix ½ cup nonfat, 2%, or whole milk with 1½ teaspoons lemon juice. You can even use the bottled kind or the plastic lemon, but fresh-squeezed is always best. This recipe is pure comfort food, and you can control the thickness of the slices. It also stores well and can be toasted over low heat or on a grill for extra flavor.

Makes 12 servings

- 2 ounces dark chocolate, chopped
- 2 medium ripe bananas, peeled
- ⅔ cup white sugar
- ¼ cup light olive oil
- 2 eggs
- 1 cup all-purpose flour (and 1 tablespoon for dusting or use a nonstick baking spray that contains flour)
- ¾ cup whole-wheat flour
- 1½ teaspoons baking powder
- ½ teaspoon baking soda
- ½ teaspoon salt
- ½ cup low-fat buttermilk
- 1 teaspoon vanilla

1. Preheat oven to 350°. Grease and flour (or spray) a 9x5-inch loaf pan and set aside.

2. In a microwave-safe bowl, heat the chopped chocolate at 10 to 15 second intervals on high, stirring often, until the chocolate is melted and smooth. Set aside to cool.

3. In a large bowl, add the bananas and sugar and mash with a fork or a potato masher until smooth. Add the olive oil and eggs and stir to combine.

4. In a medium bowl, sift together all-purpose flour, whole-wheat flour, baking powder, baking soda, and salt.

5. Add flour mixture gradually to banana mixture and stir to combine.

6. Add in buttermilk and vanilla and stir to combine.

7. Stir half the cake batter into the melted chocolate. Spoon ½ the banana batter into the bottom of the loaf pan. Add a thin layer of the chocolate batter. Repeat with remaining batters until finished.

8. Drag a knife, skewer, or end of a spoon through the batter from end to end several times to create the marble effect.

9. Bake 40 to 45 minutes, until the bread is golden and a toothpick inserted in the center comes out clean.

10. Cool 10 to 15 minutes on a rack then flip the bread out carefully and allow to cool completely.

Mini Olive Oil Cakes

Mini Olive Oil Cakes

Olive oil provides an unsurpassed taste. It makes any cake moist, flavorful, vibrant with color, and velvety in texture. These mini cakes cut out a lot of unnecessary ingredients. If you have a mini Bundt pan, these cakes come out with beautiful patterns that hold glazes or even powdered sugar perfectly. No mini Bundt? Don't worry. You can use a muffin pan or even mini loaf pans and still get the same amazing effects and flavor. These cakes can be sweet or savory by simply modifying the ingredients. The glaze on these cakes sets them apart. They are super moist on their own, but they absorb the flavors of any glaze or drizzle, or they can be soaked in, and absorb, various flavors. Try traditional glazes like vanilla, orange, lemon, mint, or almond. Or try soaking the cake in flavors like rum, lemon, or simple syrup or try topping it with fresh whipped cream, powdered sugar, candied ginger, crushed nuts, or even sweetened cereal.

Makes 12 mini cakes

- 1 tablespoon unsalted butter, melted
- 1 cup all-purpose flour, plus more for dusting, if not using nonstick spray for baking
- 1⅓ cup sugar (or Stevia)
- 2 large eggs
- ¼ cup extra-virgin olive oil
- ⅔ cup milk (whole or 2%)
- ½ teaspoon baking powder
- ½ teaspoon salt

Glaze

- 1½ cup confectioners' sugar
- 2½ to 3 tablespoons water or milk
- 1 to 2 teaspoons lemon, vanilla, almond, or orange extract

1. Preheat oven to 250°. Spray a 6- or 12-cup mini Bundt pan or muffin pan with nonstick spray for baking or coat with butter or oil lightly and sprinkle with 1-2 tablespoons of flour. Shake off the excess flour.

2. In a blender or a food processor, pulse the sugar 2 to 4 times. Add the eggs, one at a time, pulsing after each egg.

3. Gradually add the extra-virgin olive oil and milk, pulsing after each addition until the mixture is a thin batter, about 30 seconds to 1 minute.

4. In a small bowl, whisk the flour, baking powder, and salt.

5. Gradually add the flour mixture to the cake batter, pulsing after each addition just until combined.

6. Pour the batter into the prepared baking pan. Bake 25 to 30 minutes (for 6-cup Bundt pan or if using mini loaf pans) or 20 to 25 minutes (for a 12-cup Bundt pan or muffin pan). Remove from oven and cool in baking pan for 10 minutes. Loosen sides gently with a knife and invert the cakes onto a rack to cool completely.

7. Prepare the glaze: Whisk the confectioner's sugar and 2½ tablespoons water or milk and extract until smooth. Add drops of water if needed until the glaze is thick but loose enough to pour over the cakes and slide gently down the sides.

Modern Rice Pudding

Modern Rice Pudding

Rice pudding is too important of an American classic to not be enjoyed by everyone. This recipe allows anyone to enjoy the taste of rice pudding but avoid the unncessary side effects or discomforts that can come from the traditional recipe. This recipe cuts down the time it takes to make the pudding and involves less steps than traditional rice pudding. Plus, this version stays creamy in the refrigerator for several days and can be enjoyed by anyone. This pudding can be customized too—the Arborio rice can be swapped out for brown or jasmine rice, and add-ins like raisins, walnuts, mini chocolate chips, berries, or lemon zest.

Makes 4 to 6 servings

- ²⁄₃ cup Arborio rice (or Brown rice or Jasmine rice—any short grain rice works great)
- 2 cups milk (whole, 2%, or skim works best, or try Half & Half if you desire a rich, creamy texture)
- 1 vanilla bean, split lengthwise
- ½ cup sugar (turbinado, white, or a suitable substitute like Splenda works well)
- Cinnamon or unsweetened cocoa powder for dusting

1. In a medium, heavy saucepan combine rice and milk.

2. Scrape seeds from the vanilla bean and add to the rice & milk mixture. Add in the bean shell.

3. Bring the rice and milk to a boil.

4. Reduce heat to low and simmer for 25 to 30 minutes, stirring occasionally, until rice is tender.

5. Remove vanilla bean shell and mix in sugar.

6. Continue cooking until mixture thickens, about 5 to 10 minutes.

7. Serve warm or allow to cool then refrigerate for 4 to 6 hours (or overnight).

8. Consider mix-ins: raisins, chopped nuts, rum extract (1-2 teaspoons), dried fruit, pineapple chunks, flaked coconut, chia seeds, or mini chocolate chips.

9. Garnish with a dash of cinnamon or a dusting of unsweetened cocoa powder.

No-Bake Peanut Butter Chocolate Mini Bites

No-Bake Peanut Butter Chocolate Mini Bites

Peanut butter and chocolate are a perfect combination. This recipe is simply peanut and chocolate, with only a few extra ingredients added in to help it bind. Better, this recipe requires no baking or minimal clean up and can be made with ingredients you likely already have in your pantry. What keeps this healthy is portion size. These bars are purposely cut into small squares so the taste can be savored and enjoyed without having to eat a large portion of sugar. Once the whole mix is set, portions can be cut and wrapped in plastic wrap or stored in plastic containers between wax or parchment paper and taken out individually or several bites at a time. Try adding toppings like chopped peanuts, coconut flakes, or banana chips.

Makes 14 to 16 Mini Bites

Peanut Butter layer

- ¾ cup unsalted butter, melted and cooled
- 1 cup peanut butter (any brand of natural, creamy, or chunky)
- 1½ cups powdered sugar
- 1½ cups graham cracker crumbs

Chocolate layer

- 1 package (12 ounces) semi-sweet chocolate chips (any brand is fine; or any type of chocolate chip will work, depending on taste)
- ¼ cup of peanut butter (creamy is best for smoothness, but any kind can be used, including the kind used for the peanut butter layer)

1. Line a 9x13-inch baking dish with parchment paper, leaving an overhang as a sling for easy removal from the pan (or use a disposable foil pan).

2. Peanut Butter layer: Combine melted butter and peanut butter in a large

mixing bowl. Stir to combine (an electric stand-up mixer works best).

3. Add powdered sugar gradually and stir until combined.

4. Gradually add in the graham cracker crumbs (about ½ cup at a time) and mix until fully combined and smooth (no lumps or clumps in the batter).

5. Scoop peanut butter mixture into the prepared baking dish and press into an even layer. Set aside.

6. Chocolate layer: Add the chocolate chips and peanut butter to a microwave-safe bowl. Microwave in 20 to 30 second increments, stirring after each increment until the mixture is fully melted and smooth.

7. When the chocolate mixture is warm, yet easy to touch, pour over the peanut butter layer and spread into an even layer.

8. Cover tightly with aluminum foil and refrigerate 2 hours until firm and the chocolate is set.

9. Lift out using the parchment paper. Cut in 1x1- or 2x2-inch squares. Wrap each square in plastic wrap or store in an airtight container between layers of parchment paper in the refrigerator for up to a week (or freeze for several weeks).

No-Bake Truffle Cookies

No-Bake Truffle Cookies

These truffle cookies require very little prep time and use simple ingredients. This recipe relies on dates as the main ingredient, which provides lots of healthy fiber, iron, and other vitamins. These cookies are packed with flavor, fiber, and protein, with a velvety texture. The best part is they can be rolled in any number of toppings, from sweet to savory to crunchy, that elevate the flavor of these cookies.

Makes 24 cookies

- 1 cup chopped dried pitted dates
- 1 cup water
- 2 tablespoons natural honey
- 2 tablespoons natural or creamy peanut butter
- 2 tablespoons unsweetened cocoa powder
- 1 tablespoon unsalted butter
- ¼ teaspoon salt
- 1¼ cup graham cracker crumbs (about 14 to 16 crackers crushed fine)
- ½ cup old-fashioned rolled oats
- Nonstick vegetable cooking spray
- Optional toppings: coconut flakes, chopped peanuts, crushed cereal, chia seeds, chopped almonds, and granola

1. In a medium saucepan, combine dates and water. Bring to a boil then lower heat and simmer over medium heat until mixture becomes a thick paste, about 15 to 20 minutes.

2. Stir in the honey, peanut butter, cocoa powder, butter, and salt until combined. Stir in the graham cracker crumbs and oats. Remove from heat.

3. Lightly coat a baking sheet with nonstick vegetable spray.

4. Drop level tablespoons of the truffle mixture onto the prepared baking sheet. If necessary, shape dough into a rounded ball. Refrigerate until truffle dough is chilled and set, about 30 minutes.

5. Roll each chilled truffle ball in any desired topping. Return the truffle to the baking sheet and lightly press it down to slightly flatten into a cookie. Cover and refrigerate until firm, at least one hour or more.

Peanut Butter Mousse

Peanut Butter Mousse

Peanut butter is an excellent source of protein with great taste. It's also a versatile food that can be bought fat free or low fat, all natural or chunky and used in sweet, savory, or ethnic recipes. This recipe is an easy way to have dessert or a snack without spending a lot of time baking or preparing. In fact, there's no baking at all! The ingredients are things most people have available and the flavor profile can be changed simply by changing the toppings. It holds up well for several days in the refrigerator and is best when served cold.

Makes 4 to 6 servings

- 1 cup heavy cream
- 1 8-ounce package light cream cheese, softened
- 1 cup creamy peanut butter (any brand)
- 1 teaspoon vanilla extract
- 2 cups powdered sugar (confectioner's)
- Optional toppings: crushed pretzels, chopped peanuts, grated chocolate, chocolate curls, mini chocolate chips, or ½ teaspoon of chocolate cookie crumbs

1. In the bowl of a stand-up mixer or in a large bowl, use the whisk attachment or an electric mixer and medium-high speed to whip heavy cream until stiff. Set aside.

2. In a second bowl, add cream cheese, peanut butter, and vanilla to bowl and beat on low- medium speed until combined.

3. Slowly add in powdered sugar and beat to combine. If too stiff, add in extra tablespoons of heavy cream or milk.

4. Gently fold the whipped cream into the peanut butter mixture and stir to combine. Do not overmix.

5. Spoon mousse into individual serving dishes, ramekins, or a glass bowl. Refrigerate for at least 1 to 2 hours or overnight.

6. Top with crushed pretzels, chopped peanuts, grated chocolate, chocolate curls, mini chocolate chips, or ½ teaspoon of chocolate cookie crumbs.

Peanut Butter Pretzel Bars

Peanut Butter Pretzel Bars

These bars are perfect as a snack, a power or energy boost, a great dessert to share, or even as a quick on-the-go meal. Even better, these bars can be made ahead and frozen for up to 2 months or stored in the refrigerator for 5 days or a week. The crust is so simple to make with mini pretzels or use pretzel sticks or rods. These bars can be changed up simply by adding dried fruit or different chocolate or using different peanut butters or brands of peanut butter.

Makes 16 large or 25 small squares

- 3 cups mini pretzels (unsalted best)
- ½ cup unsalted butter, melted
- 2 tablespoons sugar
- 1 14-ounce can sweetened condensed milk, divided
- ¼ cup peanut butter (smooth or creamy works best)
- ¾ cup peanut butter chips
- 1½ cups unsweetened coconut flakes
- ½ cup mini chocolate chips (optional)

1. Preheat oven to 350°. Spray an 8x8- or 9x13-inch baking dish with vegetable spray. Line the sides and bottom of the baking dish with parchment paper, allowing the edges of the paper to overhang.

2. Prepare the crust: Add pretzels to the bowl of a food processor and pulse until they become fine crumbs (or use a resealable plastic bag and crush the pretzels with a rolling pin or heavy can until crumbled). Add in the butter and sugar and pulse until combined (or add the crumbs to a bowl and stir until combined).

3. Press the pretzel mix into the bottom of the prepared baking dish. Press firmly, using your fingers or the back of a measuring cup, so the crumbs

get compacted into the bottom and corners of the baking dish.

4. Bake the crust for 15 minutes. Remove from the oven and allow to cool on a wire rack.

5. In a microwave-safe bowl, combine half the sweetened condensed milk and peanut butter. Microwave on high 20 to 30 seconds (or more if needed), stirring often until mixture is smooth.

6. Spread half the coconut flakes onto the cooled pretzel crust, followed by half the peanut butter chips and chocolate chips, if using.

7. Pour the peanut butter mixture over the top then repeat with layers of coconut, peanut butter chips, and chocolate chips, if using.

8. Drizzle the remaining peanut butter mixture across the top.

9. Bake 35 to 40 minutes, until the edges are golden brown. Remove from the oven and cool completely on a wire rack.

10. Once cooled, use the parchment paper to lift the cooled mixture out of the baking dish and onto a cutting board. Use a serrated knife to cut the mixture into small or large bars.

11. Store in an airtight container for 5 to 7 days or refrigerate for up to 1 week. Freeze bars for up to 2 months.

Saturated Berries

Saturated Berries

Berries contain multiple vitamins and essential fiber that aid digestion and promote overall health. They're great plain but ideal to add to salads, yogurt, muffins, or bread. This recipe intensifies their flavors and is a healthy alternative to prepare berries that make them perfect to use as a topping, a mix in for yogurt, oatmeal, or smoothies, or on their own as a snack or dessert.

Makes 2 to 4 servings

- 1 to 2 cups of berries—strawberries, blueberries, blackberries, raspberries, or a combination of all of them
- 1 tablespoon of Stevia (i.e., natural sugar substitute) or turbinado sugar
- 2 teaspoons balsamic vinegar

1. Clean the berries with cold water and pat dry. (If using strawberries, cut or hull the berries.)

2. Add the Stevia to the berries. Toss to coat.

3. Add the balsamic vinegar and toss to combine.

4. Refrigerate the berries for 6 to 8 hours (overnight is best).

5. Serve over ice cream, frozen yogurt, waffles, pancakes, or polenta slices. Or serve as a dessert topped with whipped cream and garnished with mint.

The Best Man's Bites

The Best Man's Bites

This recipe came about as a way to make a quick snack for the Best Man at a wedding to have in his pocket for an emergency snack during a long ceremony. This recipe relies on how well sweet and savory flavors work together to produce a delicious treat. It incorporates peanut butter plus pretzels and the slight tang of bittersweet chocolate. A simple touch of brown sugar and time baked in the oven turns this commonly frozen dessert into a warm, delectable treat that can be eaten as a dessert or snack. It also adds a nice touch of protein.

Makes 14 to 16 servings

- ½ cup natural peanut butter (any brand)
- 1 cup unsalted butter, softened
- ½ cup light brown sugar, packed
- 1 teaspoon vanilla extract
- 2 cups all-purpose flour
- 30 to 36 pretzel sticks
- 3 ounces bittersweet chocolate

1. Preheat oven to 350°.

2. In a large mixing bowl or the bowl of a stand-up mixer, beat the peanut butter, butter, and brown sugar until creamy.

3. Add vanilla and beat to combine.

4. Gradually add in the flour, beating on low after each addition.

5. Press the dough evenly into a lightly greased 8x8- or 9x13-inch baking dish or onto a 15x30-inch baking sheet.

6. Gently press the pretzel sticks into the dough, making even lines down the length of the dough. Use more pretzel sticks if necessary, depending on the size baking dish or pan used, to cover the entire length of the dough.

7. Bake 13 to 14 minutes, until the edges are golden and the center is set. Remove from the oven and cool.

8. Melt chocolate in a heat-safe bowl in the microwave on high heat; stir often until all the chocolate is melted. Drizzle across the cooled, baked dough.

9. Slice into squares. Wrap individual squares in plastic wrap or store in an airtight container in the refrigerator for up to 1 week.

A Note from the Author

The information and recipes in this book are not intended to replace the advice, instructions, or plan of care developed by a licensed health care practitioner. Women, or anyone embarking on a journey toward healthier living, should consult their health care practitioner and follow their specific instructions or recommendations. Anyone with a known allergy to any ingredient, or an aversion to specific ingredients, should avoid specific recipes.

Acknowledgements

The author gratefully acknowledges the incredible team who assisted in some way to the Prenatal Possibilities brand and the creation of this book. My sincerest thanks to Dr. Lettie Conrad, Alicia Warren, Tracey Molineux, Sarah Horvath, Elizabeth Kemmerly, Peter Smith, Laura Rembold, Dawn Dowdle, Level Best Books, Erica Scalise, Nadine Drake, Nick Benedetto and NBPro Media Productions.

About the Author

Paul Quinn is a Certified Nurse Midwife with over 30 years of experience in women's healthcare. Holding a PhD in nursing, he is an accomplished researcher in women's health and is the author of *Sexually Transmitted Diseases: Your Questions Answered, Birth Control: Your Questions Answered,* and *Teen Pregnancy: Your Questions Answered.*

SOCIAL MEDIA HANDLES:
  Instagram: drpaulquinn
  Facebook: Paul Quinn

AUTHOR WEBSITE: www.prenatalpossibilities.com

Also by Paul Quinn

Sexually Transmitted Diseases: Your Questions Answered (ABC-CLIO/Greenwood)

Birth Control: Your Questions Answered (ABC-CLIO/Greenwood)

Teen Pregnancy: Your Questions Answered (ABC-CLIO/Greenwood)

Ingram Content Group UK Ltd.
Milton Keynes UK
UKHW050642060423
419704UK00011B/56